Physical Characteristics of the Beagle

(from the American Kennel Club breed standard)

W9-BLC-483

Body: Back short, muscular and strong. Loin broad and slightly arched, and the ribs well sprung, giving abundance of lung room.

Tail: Set moderately high; carried gaily, but not turned forward over the back; with slight curve; short as compared with size of the hound; with brush.

Hips and Thighs: Hips and thighs strong and well muscled, giving abundance of propelling power.

Coat: A close, hard, hound coat of medium length.

Color: Any true hound color.

Varieties: Thirteen Inch—which shall be for hounds not exceeding 13 inches in height. Fifteen Inch—which shall be for hounds over 13 but not exceeding 15 inches in height.

Feet: Close, round and firm. Pad full and hard.

Beagle

by Evelyn Elizabeth Lanyon

Contents

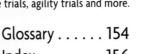
KENNEL CLUB BOOKS: **BEAGLE**
ISBN: **1-59378-234-9**

Copyright © 1999 • **Revised American Edition: Copyright © 2003**
Kennel Club Books, Inc., 308 Main Street, Allenhurst, NJ 07711 USA
Cover Design Patented: US 6,435,559 B2 • Printed in South Korea

Photographs by Carol Ann Johnson with additional photo by:
Norvia Behling, T. J. Calhoun, Carolina Biological Supply, Doskocil,
Isabelle Français, James Hayden-Yoav, James R. Hayden, RBP, Bill Jonas,
Dwight R. Kuhn, Dr. Dennis Kunkel, Nancy Liguori, Mikki Pet Products, Phototake, Jean
Claude Revy, Dr. Andrew Spielman, Karen Taylor, Alice van Kempen and C. James Webb.

Illustrations by Renée Low

Beagle

Beagles are excellent as pets for people of all ages, as show dogs and as hunting dogs. They are hardy and versatile, and they love people.

HISTORY OF THE
BEAGLE

The origin of the Beagle, like that of most other hound breeds, cannot be positively traced; it appears buried in antiquity. In the second century AD, *Onomasticon*, a Greek dictionary in ten books by Iulius Pollux, mentions the dog being used by man for hunting purposes about 1300 BC. The ancient Greek author Xenophon made references in his writings of about 450 BC to small hounds used to hunt hare on foot. While no formal name was given to these small hounds, they were undoubtedly the prognosticators of the dog we have come to know today as the Beagle.

Early man hunted animals for survival itself but, through the centuries, hunting evolved from a means to sustain life into a sport. The landed gentry and nobility of England, as early as the fourteenth century, participated in blood sports as a social activity. They used horses and large and small hounds, along with small terriers,

Alert, compact and lively, with exceptional scenting skills, the Beagle was a favored hunting companion of royalty and now is a familiar face to dog lovers everywhere.

Evolutionists agree that all breeds of domestic dog have developed from the wolf.

CLUB OBJECTIVES

England's Beagle Club's objectives and aims were published in 1899 and they still remain unchanged: "It keeps wide open its doors and welcomes alike to the fold the Master of Beagles who wishes to maintain or form his Pack on ancient lines; the shooting man who keeps a few couples for driving out the rabbits, or putting up the pheasant; the drag hunter who gets an afternoon's healthy exercise with the pleasure of seeing hounds work and hearing hound music; the exhibitor who finds pleasure in breeding for perfection, so far as looks go, and performs most useful work by making the beauty of the breed more generally known; the lady who finds the Beagle the most intelligent and interesting of pets; last, but certainly not the least, the old sportsman whose sporting days are over, who has a keen remembrance of what has been and joins in, whilst his recollections and experiences are of inestimable value to a younger generation. All these are now united in the same effort."

in the pursuit of deer, fox, badger and hare.

Selection for desired physical characteristics and mental traits to suit a purpose is how the various purebred dog breeds came into being. In prehistoric times, the breeder was the caveman looking for a dog whose basic instincts were strong, and he used the best of these dogs to assist him in finding and catching food. Later, the breeder was the farmer, who found that keeping a hardy and energetic dog around helped keep meat on the family's table. The caveman and, much later, the farmer both followed the dogs on foot.

Later, when the Beagle was kept by the British aristocracy, stockmen were employed and it was their job to make the selection of stock. The aristocracy, having the wealth to do so, kept large numbers of hounds together in packs; the evenness of type in these packs was highly regarded. The terrain varied from county to county throughout England and so the desired type varied from pack to pack to serve the challenges of the local hunt. The groups of wealthy sportsmen usually followed the hounds on horseback.

By repeatedly selecting desirable characteristics and traits to suit the purpose at hand, the breeder, whether the caveman, the farmer, the stockman, etc., fixed type within the dogs and these small hounds eventually were refined and bred with some consistency.

During the Middle Ages in England, there were two varieties of hound said to be quite numerous, known as Northern Hounds and Southern Hounds. There also were hounds of a larger type used for trailing deer, probably the Foxhound, and others of a smaller type used for trailing hare, thought to be

The Foxhound, though much larger than the Beagle, seems to figure in the background of the Beagle. The American breed is lankier than the English.

was the swiftest. There is also mention of North-Country Beagles by seventeenth-century writers, including William Somerville (1675–1742), who refer to this dog as being fast and more slender than the Cotswold Beagle. Perhaps the Northern Hound and the North-Country Beagle are one and the same; it would seem so.

So what breeds of dog were put together to produce the Beagle? Some believe that the breed resulted from a crossing of the Harrier with the old South of England or Southern Hound. In some instances, they were referred to as "little Harriers."

The Belvoir pack, with both Beagles and English Fox-hounds, was one of the most important packs in England. It is seen in this historic photo, moving off after the Meet at Croxton Park, near Grantham. In the background is the noteworthy edifice known as the Olde Croxton Abbey.

Harriers and Beagles.

Little has been written to describe the Northern Hound but William Youatt, in his book *The Dog*, published in 1846, mentions "the shallow-flewed, more contracted lip of the Northern dogs" and claimed that this type

TYPE AND STANDARD

"Type" refers to those characteristic qualities distinguishing a breed, the embodiment of a breed standard's essentials. The standard is a written description of the ideal dog of each recognized breed, written to serve as a word pattern by which dogs are judged at shows.

Foxhounds and Beagles are similar in many traits and abilities as well as looks, despite the large difference in size.

Most scholars seem to support the theory that the modern Beagle came down for the most part from the Harrier. Selection for the smaller dog, litter after litter, over and over again, fixed the size—what was once called a small Foxhound or a small Harrier is known today as the Beagle.

During the seventeenth century, Beagles were mentioned by many different but similar names: Northern Hounds and Southern Hounds; Rough-Coated and Smooth-Coated Beagles. The Southern Hound was described by Gervase Markham as having "a longer nose, ears and flews more shallow, his general appearance slender and greyhound-like. They had good noses and were fast but in respect of mouth they were a little sharp, with no real depth of tone or music." William Youatt, in his book *The Dog,* agreed with Stonehenge (J. H. Walsh, a noted dog authority of the Victorian era) and felt that the Harrier crossed with the old Southern Hound was the combination that produced the Beagle.

In *Cynographia Britannica,* published about 1800, there are descriptions of Southern Beagles and Northern Beagles. The small hounds were described as varieties generally distinguished by the parts of the country in which they were bred, which lends support to the quote credited to William Somerville at about the same time, "A different Hound for every different chase; select with judgement."

Northern Beagles were commonly wire-haired, straight-limbed and better formed in their shoulders and haunches, and endured bad weather and lengthy exercise better than the Southern Beagle. William Somerville described the Cotswold Beagle, whom he credited as producing some of his best Harriers when

WHAT'S IN A NAME?

The origin of the name Beagle is not certain, but there are a number of theories. *Squire of Low Degree*, first published in 1475, is the first mention of the Beagle (by name) in English literature. "With theyr beagles in that place and seven score raches at his rechase." Some people believe the word to be derived from the Old English word *begle*. The French *beigh* and the Celtic *beag* are also possibilities—all mean "small."

crossed with the old Southern Hound.

The author Beckford wrote in about 1750 of Fox-Beagles and described them as being exceptionally lively in temperament as well as fleet of foot. He records that he crossed his Harriers with them to give more dash and drive. Also mentioned are Rough-Coated Beagles and Wire-Haired Beagles, who almost certainly are the same, since both were found mainly in Devon in the South of England and in nearby Wales. William Youatt claimed the Wire-Haired

This historic illustration was originally captioned: "Apparently the hare has passed through a wood and the scent has been lost, the Beagles not knowing which way to go."

Beagle was the stronger, stouter and better variety. Those familiar with both Fox Terriers and Beagles realize that there is cause to believe that Fox Terrier blood exists in present-day Beagles,

THE HARRIER

The Harrier is a small edition of the Foxhound but some authorities believe he is a cross between the Beagle and the St. Hubert Hound (a Bloodhound-like dog of smaller stature.) Stonehenge thought the Harrier came from the Southern Hound with a little Greyhound thrown in.

Some believe the Harrier (shown here) to be the Beagle's direct ancestor—the "small Harriers" of yesteryear are today's Beagle.

13

This Dennis Moss photo from the early 1900s was captioned: "The Royal Agricultural College at Cirencester has one of the best packs of Beagles in England. The pack is here seen moving off after a Meet outside the College…"

WHAT A DRAG!

Since the modern-day enthusiast is neither likely to find a field nearby with hare lollygagging about nor to wish to see a hare killed just for sport, you can easily create a "drag" with an artificial scent as a substitute for a hare. Mix together half an ounce of oil of aniseed, a quarter of an ounce of essential oil of valerian and an ounce and a quarter of castor oil, and dip a cloth in the mixture. Tie a string to the soaked cloth and drag it through a field, occasionally redipping the cloth to keep the scent strong. Then turn your Beagle loose and watch the action!

perhaps the source of the Beagle's legendary stubbornness.

Kerry Beagles are also mentioned repeatedly by scholars and were quite different from the general idea of what a Beagle should look like: upstanding, rather lightly built, black-and-tan and in many ways resembling the Bloodhound. This breed was said to have existed in Southern Ireland for hundreds of years, and the Ryan family of Scarteen claims to have owned them since 1735. They were not seen in England until the early twentieth century. Some think the present-day Beagle gets his keen nose from the Kerry Beagle, who was in color and general appearance a miniature Bloodhound.

Stonehenge, in his *Manual of British Sports* (1861), gave the varieties of Beagles as follows: "First, the medium Beagle, which may be either heavy and Southern-like or light and Northern-like; second, the dwarf or lap-dog Beagle; third the Fox Beagle, and fourth the rough or Terrier Beagle."

Through the centuries, British royalty has favored the Beagle. During the reign of Henry VIII, Beagles are said to have been popular. There exists written evidence of Beagles during the reign of Henry's daughter, Elizabeth I (1558–1603), as well as pictures that depicted members of her Court hunting with Beagles. There is also a portrait of Queen Elizabeth I with a Beagle at her side. Interestingly, the Beagles in Elizabethan times were very small. Described as dwarfs, Pygmy Beagles or Pocket Beagles, they ranged in height from 8 to 10 inches at the top of the shoulder and were small enough to be occasionally carried to the chase in a pair of panniers on the horse's back.

Another royal who favored the Beagle is King James I (1566–1625), who enjoyed the sport of hunting the hare with his pack of Beagles. A century later, during the reign of King George IV (1762–1830), English Beagles were described as rough-coated or

smooth-coated, with King George preferring the smooth-coated Beagle. While Prince of Wales, he enjoyed hunting with his pack of dwarf Beagles. These very small

This famous painting by Maud Earl shows Miss Oughton's pack of Beagles, about 1899, discovering the hare when least expecting to find it.

KERRY BEAGLES

Early in the twentieth century, a group of Irish emigrants took their Kerry Beagles to the United States, where they contributed to the development of several American varieties of hound. In Ireland, breeders have stirred a resurgence of interest in this active and friendly dog. The Kerry Beagle is still used for hare hunting, and the rising popularity of drag trials in Ireland has created a new activity for the breed. The modern Kerry Beagle comes in traditional hound colors, stands about 22–26 inches at the top of the shoulder and weighs 45–60 lbs.

Beagles did not enjoy popularity much past this period.

Toward the end of the nineteenth century, organized dog activities began. The aristocracy, long committed to the hunt, owned packs of Foxhounds, Harriers and Beagles. They hunted mostly on horseback, chasing fox with the larger Foxhounds and Harriers, and hare with the smaller Beagle. "Beagling" is described as the art of hunting the hare in its natural surroundings with a pack of small hounds that rely solely on their noses to work out the intricate paths the hare has taken. Beagling became popular with the commoner, too, since the smaller Beagle could be followed on foot.

England's Kennel Club was formed in 1873 and dog shows were then held on a regular basis. The first recorded mention of Beagles being shown in England was at the Tunbridge Wells Dog Society Show on August 21 and

This Keystone photo (circa 1901) is entitled "Cubbing." The caption reads: "Before fox-hunting starts in all seriousness, early Meets are held at which the stock is thinned down and the foxes are dispersed. These early Meets go by the name of Cubbing, and the Fife Foxhound Pack is seen on its way to the first draw."

22, 1884, with eight or nine Beagles entered. There was a separate class for Beagles of any size, and the best hound under 14 inches in this class was presented with a silver cup and a hunting horn.

The Beagle Club of England was formed in 1890, held its first show in 1896 and published its first *Year Book* in 1897. World War I (1914–1918) stopped much of the Beagle activities, but interest increased again during the two successive decades. World War II (1939–1945) again interfered, and Viscount Chelmsford is credited with restarting the club.

The UK's Association of Masters of Harriers and Beagles was founded in 1891. The association's members were limited to those who were keeping, or had kept, registered packs that regularly hunt the hare. The object of both clubs was to further the interest of the Beagles. In the early 1950s, there was a great deal of renewed interest in the Beagle that carries through to this day. Since 1962, a number of regional Beagle clubs have formed around the British Isles.

Today, Beagles have classes at most of the Open Shows in the United Kingdom and at all of the General Championship Shows that come under the rules and regulations of The Kennel Club. Entries are large, often 100 or

more, and sometimes twice that number.

THE BEAGLE ON THE CONTINENT

In France, during the reign of the Bourbons (1589–1848), the lavishness of the chase was unparalleled. At Chantilly, where Prince Louis Henry de Bourbon resided, records of the sport have been preserved. The records from 1748

One of the attractions of owning a high-quality Beagle is that it can be shown in addition to being a family pet.

The upper photo shows a disorganized pack of Beagles heading in every direction, trying to pick up a scent. The lower photo shows the dogs on the scent, with the Master keeping up with the pack.

to 1779 show that 77,750 hare were accounted for in the chase, as well as 3,364 stags and hinds.

The Foxhound is thought to have descended from four different types of French hounds. In George Turberville's *Art of Venerie*, written around the reign of Queen Elizabeth I, the French hound types were described, "...the White, used principally for stag hunting; the Fallow, used on all sorts of game, mainly the stag; the Dun, used more frequently than any other hound breed and good on any game and the Black or St. Hubert's, of many colors and no doubt the forebear of the Bloodhound and the Southern Hound." The Southern Hound, when crossed with the smaller Harrier (often called a small edition of the Foxhound), is thought by many experts to be the forebear of the Beagle.

As in the breed's British homeland, fanciers of the Beagle on the Continent enjoyed the merry little hunting hound as the all-around dog, a devoted hunter on a variety of game as well as an attractive companion for the drawing room. In modern times, the Beagle's popularity has remained strong and the breed a major entry at dog exhibitions through Europe.

THE BEAGLE IN THE UNITED STATES

Beginning in Colonial times, Europeans emigrating to America brought dogs with them, some to serve as guards, some to pull carts and others to secure game for food. Some of these dogs were brought because of their innate ability to scent, to trail and to capture game.

The first recorded mention of the Beagle was in Joseph Barrow Felt's *History of Ipswich, Essex, and Hamilton*, published in 1834. The book was based in part upon early town records and, in the records for the year 1642, the Beagle is mentioned as having helped local hunters to keep wolves from the town.

Prior to the Civil War (1861–1865), hunters in the Southern states used small hunting hounds, including

Beagles, to pursue fox and hare. During the war, almost all hunting ceased, but, after the war, interest again picked up. Wanting to improve the quality of their stock, some more affluent hunters imported Beagles from Europe.

In the early 1870s, General Richard Rowett from Illinois

Beagles were shipped to America as early as 1642. They have been a favorite breed ever since.

19

Beagle

became highly interested in Beagles. He imported dogs from England and from them bred what fanciers during those times thought were very good representatives of the breed. The Rowett Beagles were known for their consistency of type, evenness of markings and ability in the field.

Another noted breeder of that period was Mr. Norman Elmore, who imported some influential dogs in the development of his Elmore line. Ringwood and Countess were two of these imports, with Ringwood being used at stud extensively and his offspring often taken to the Rowett strain. The two gentlemen, General Rowett and Mr. Elmore, worked together and the two strains produced what many thought were the best Beagles of the time.

About 1880, Mr. Arnold of Rhode Island imported a pack of Beagles from the Royal Rock line in northern England. Approximately six years later, Mr. James L. Kernochan imported another pack from England, all of which had considerable influence on the quality of Beagles in America. From these times forward, the popularity of the Beagle rose steadily.

In 1885, a dog named Blunder was the first Beagle to be registered in the Stud Book of the American Kennel Club. The National Beagle Club was founded in 1888 and the club held the first field trial for the breed two years later in Hyannis, Massachusetts, with an entry of 18. It is believed that the first American standard for the breed was drawn up by General Rowett, Mr. Norman Elmore and a Dr. L. H. Twaddell.

On December 21, 1901, Ch. Windholme's Bangle, a five-year-old bitch owned by Mr. Harry T. Peters, became the breed's first all-breed Best in Show winner. By 1917, the popularity of the Beagle as a show dog was evidenced by an entry of 75 at America's premier show, the Westminster Kennel Club event, held in New York City. At this show, Beagles enjoyed great success, winning first in the Sporting Group (there was no Hound Group at that time), as well as Best Sporting Brace and Best Sporting Team in Show. It is interesting to note that it was at this event that Beagles were first shown as two varieties based on size: one class for Beagles 13 inches and under, and the other for Beagles over 13 inches but under 15 inches. The breed has been shown in America in these two separate varieties ever since.

Interest and enthusiasm for this clever little hunter have never waned in America. Today, the Beagle is one of the most popular all-around breeds, as a companion, an enthusiastic hunter and trailer and a highly competitive member of the Hound Group.

American Beagles are categorized by size. The line of demarcation is 13 inches. Beagles below 13 inches and those above (but less than 15) are exhibited in two separate categories.

BEAGLE

The reasons for the Beagle's continued popularity are varied and due to the Beagle's being truly a versatile dog—one that has fulfilled many different roles. First and foremost, he was essentially a gundog, a true sporting hound. Secondly, he was a specialist on hare, found abundantly in the British Isles, and cottontail rabbits, which are prolific in the US. Thirdly, his versatility as a hunter shone in that he could be used on almost any type of upland game and was particularly effective on squirrel and pheasant. And last, but not least, he was and still is today a merry, affectionate and loyal little dog, making him a favorite as a household pet and companion for the family.

All puppies are cute, but there is nothing quite so adorable as a Beagle puppy. The breed standard of the American Kennel Club defines the Beagle's expression as soft, gentle and pleading. I particularly like the word "pleading," as it is that look that makes it almost impossible to turn away from a litter of Beagle pups when all of them seem to be saying, "Please, take me home!" Those big brown eyes and floppy ears can melt a stone.

VIRTUES OF THE BEAGLE
The Beagle is a breed that fits easily into most households. He wants to please those he loves and be in their company as much as possible, thriving on being with his special people.

Beagles are amenable to training but will never be the precision worker that the average Doberman Pinscher or Shetland Sheepdog easily becomes. When you say, "Come," the Beagle's tendency is to reply, "Yes, in a minute," and carry on with what he is doing. Since the Beagle yearns to please, he learns what makes you happy and, thus, him

FAMOUS BEAGLES

Famous Beagles include two Beagles owned by the 36th President, Lyndon Baines Johnson (1963–1969). The dogs were named Him and Her, and were frequent visitors to the Oval Office in the White House. Another famous Beagle is the popular cartoon character Snoopy of the *Peanuts* gang, created by the late Californian Charles Schultz.

inherent desire to hunt and trail, and his body construction, he is an athletic and functional hound. He can jump up on your lap and into your car, go for long walks on lead and join you on runs through the woods or along the beach.

He is an easy keeper, too, requiring just the standard diet of quality dog food, and, with that nice short coat, there is little grooming to be done. He requires an occasional bath and a weekly grooming, including brushing and combing, to keep the loose hair in check and his nails trimmed back.

On the downside, Beagle stubbornness is legendary. The Beagle needs an owner who is gentle but firm, tolerant and persistent...someone who won't lose his temper when the dog wantonly disobeys, someone who enjoys a challenge!

Beagles can make themselves at home anywhere. A soft rug to lie on, food and water...what more could a Beagle ask for? They also need love, attention, training and activity.

comfortable, and will strive to maintain that status quo. He will be just as obedient as necessary to keep on your good side, but, being a Beagle, he will think of some innovative tricks to keep you laughing and amused. Life with a Beagle is always fun!

The Beagle comes in a handy size, usually ranging between 10–16 inches at the top of the shoulder, although the AKC disqualifies those over 15 inches from showing. He is squarely built, meaning that the length of his body measured from his chest to his rump is approximately equal to his height from the ground to the top of his shoulders. With his

BREEDERS ONLY

Your children do not need to witness the miracle of birth by breeding their beloved pet. This knowledge can be gained from trips to the library, books and videotapes. There are too many unwanted puppies in the world right now and unless your Beagle is of top show potential and been specifically placed with you for breeding purposes, it is best to leave the breeding of Beagles to knowledgeable, committed and responsible breeders.

HOUND GROUP

The Beagle is a member of the American Kennel Club's Hound Group, which includes sighthounds (Afghan Hounds, Borzoi, Greyhounds, etc.), who hunt by sight, and scenthounds (Beagles, Bassets, Bloodhounds, Foxhounds, Harriers, etc.), who hunt by scent. The larger Foxhound (American and English), medium-sized Harrier and smaller Beagle are similar in appearance yet are easily recognized due to their differences in height.

The Beagle's "music" is exactly that—music to some but noise to others. A lonely Beagle is going to howl and, in some urban settings, this does not make for good neighbor relations.

WHO IS THE IDEAL OWNER?

The Beagle, due to his inherent easy and steady disposition, fits into most family situations. It doesn't take an overly dominant owner to become master of this dog. The Beagle, like almost every other breed, needs to be a full-fledged member of the household. He will do well with an owner who takes him for long daily walks, brings him on trips in the family car and includes him in watching television in the evenings.

A working couple can provide a good home for a Beagle if the dog is not left outside when they are at home and is included, whenever possible, in the evening and weekend activities.

He generally does well with children of all ages, provided he has been raised with them and that the youngsters are kind, gentle and considerate of their dog. Children and dogs go together well, provided the children are aware that the dog is a "person in a fur coat," not a teddy bear or a doll.

WHAT DOES THE BEAGLE REQUIRE?

The household with someone at home during the day is ideal for any dog, making socialization and house-training a breeze. But in these modern times, when so many couples work and the children are off at school, some planning must be done to accommodate the puppy while he is left alone. No puppy should be left loose in a house; even having him closed in the kitchen or another room is not an ideal situation. A lonely puppy becomes a bored puppy, and pretty soon damage is done to his surroundings. This isn't good for the furnishings nor is it good for the puppy, as many things that the puppy may get into can cause great harm and big veterinary bills. You will want to learn all about the proper use of a crate as a tool for training and housebreaking puppies.

Every dog in an urban setting must have a fenced enclosure. No dog can be expected to stay within the confines of his own property without a fence, nor to safely run loose in a neighborhood, and Beagles are no exception. There are too many vehicles about, among other dangers, to chance a dog's being loose on the streets.

All walks must be on a leash and collar. Any time he is off-lead, he must be far, far away from traffic as his natural curiosity, keen sense of smell and love of the chase will cause him to throw

NEUTERING

The advantage of neutering a male puppy is that it often dramatically reduces any chance of prostate cancer in the older dog. Does neutering a male significantly change his personality? No. Experts agree that the neutered male dog makes an excellent companion and about the only difference noted is that the pup exhibits fewer "macho" tendencies, such as lifting his leg on the furniture or mounting people, furniture, etc.

The Beagle, due to his wonderful disposition, gets along with all members of the family under almost every circumstance. Here the youngsters are attempting to teach "give me your paw" using a treat as a reward.

25

caution to the wind and just keep going, with or without his owner.

No dog wants to be locked away when the family is home. A Beagle who is included whenever possible in family activities will be a happy, well-adjusted Beagle.

BEAGLE HEALTH CONCERNS

Hypothyroidism (low thyroid function) is a fairly common health problem in all dogs, purebred and crossbred alike, which affects many older Beagles. Most dogs are born with normal thyroid function, but many become hypothyroid as they age. There are two causes of this condition, one being auto-immune thyroid disease and the other, more common, being idiopathic hypothyroidism.

The good news about the latter hypothyroidism is that the disease is easily diagnosed with a blood test, and treatment is easy and inexpensive, simply a small pill taken once or twice daily. Common indicators of hypothyroidism are lethargy, tendency towards obesity, increased sensitivity to heat and cold, bilateral hair loss and bilateral blackening of skin, particularly on the abdomen and thighs. Hypothyroidism can also adversely affect reproduction.

Back problems in dogs are as common as they are in humans, and Beagles are known to suffer from them. There are many

reasons for dogs to have back problems (extending from the thoracic vertebrae through the lumbar vertebrae to the coccygeal vertebrae region), including familial as well as environmental causes. Dogs with skeletal problems that affect their flexibility and movement should not be used for breeding.

Additionally, great care should be given to keeping your Beagle slim and trim, with just a nice layer of fat and muscle covering the ribs. Ideally he should look like a lean, hard athlete, capable of doing the job for which he was bred.

Common symptoms of back problems can be reluctance to go up and down stairs or in and out of your car, shivering, hiding, lack of appetite and, in the extreme, hunched posture or partial or complete paralysis of the hindquarters. Any and all symptoms require immediate attention from a veterinarian.

Beagles need exercise and they love to run. In order to give your Beagle some much appreciated off-lead exercise, do so in a safe area and only if your dog has learned to come reliably when called.

in eating things that are not found in their food bowls, resulting, of course, in gastrointestinal distress. Dogs who are known to have stolen from the kitchen table, raided the trash or pilfered from the clothes hamper must be watched for signs of distress: lack of appetite, vomiting, diarrhea or obstruction of the bowels. Please remember that puppies and adults alike are known to swallow items that are not radiodense; objects like a lady's pantyhose or lingerie items will not show up on a radiograph but can totally obstruct the intestine. It is best to seek professional help as soon as distress is noted.

Spending quality time with your Beagle will give you a chance to familiarize yourself with your pet's daily habits, making it easier to recognize when something is not right.

Canine epilepsy (a seizure disorder) is another disease that affects Beagles. Extensive research has been done on the inheritance of epilepsy, and pedigree analysis demonstrates that it is a familial pattern of inheritance (occurring in more members of a family than expected by chance). A question to ask any breeder you are visiting about his line is, "Have any of your dogs suffered from seizures?" It is important for you to know that a responsible breeder would not breed from stock affected by epilepsy. There are other reasons for seizures besides epilepsy, but any seizure would be cause to see a veterinarian immediately for a complete diagnostic check-up.

"Garbage-can enteritis" is a term given to dogs who indulge

SPAYING

The advantage of spaying a bitch puppy before her first heat cycle (estrus) is that it greatly reduces any possibility of developing mammary cancer. It is common for the first heat cycle to occur anytime after five months of age and is indicated by a swollen vulva and a bloody discharge. While previous thinking indicated that a bitch should have one heat cycle before being spayed, that philosophy has changed. Surgical sterilization of puppies, male and females alike, is taking place earlier and earlier and has been successfully done as early as six weeks of age.

BEAGLE

WHAT IS THE BREED STANDARD?

The standard is a description of the ideal dog, and, in this case, the ideal Beagle. A standard is written for every recognized breed to serve as a set of guidelines for breeders and a "word picture" by which dogs are judged at shows.

The dog show judge must have a picture of the ideal Beagle firmly set in his mind's eye and, when he sees such a dog, he must quickly recognize the dog as the best before him. How a judge places the dogs in the class is based on how closely each dog resembles this written ideal.

The standard is full of terms that are known within the canine world and are understood by judges, stockmen and breeders, but not necessarily by the pet-owning public. These terms are not always described correctly in a standard English dictionary but are found routinely in breed books or general dog books like the canine dictionary *Canine Terminology*, written by Australian author and dog judge Harold R. Spira. As well as the standard mentioned here, the American Kennel Club (AKC) also sets forth criteria for judging packs of Beagles.

THE AMERICAN KENNEL CLUB STANDARD FOR THE BEAGLE

Head: The skull should be fairly long, slightly domed at occiput, with cranium broad and full. *Ears*—Ears set on moderately low, long, reaching when drawn out nearly, if not quite, to the end of the nose; fine in texture, fairly broad—with almost entire absence of erectile power—setting close to the head, with the forward edge slightly inturning to the cheek—rounded at tip. *Eyes*—Eyes large, set well apart—soft and houndlike—expression gentle and pleading; of a brown or hazel color. *Muzzle*—Muzzle of medium length—straight and square-cut—the stop moderately defined. *Jaws*—Level. Lips free from flews; nostrils large and open. *Defects*—A very flat skull, narrow across the top; excess of dome, eyes small, sharp and terrierlike, or prominent and protruding; muzzle long, snipy or cut away decidedly below the eyes, or very short. Roman-nosed, or upturned, giving a dish-face expression. Ears

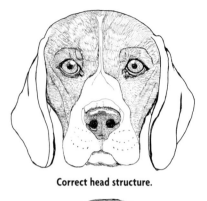

Correct head structure.

Incorrect ears; too short.

A beautiful champion-quality Beagle.

Shoulders and Chest: Shoulders sloping—clean, muscular, not heavy or loaded—conveying the idea of freedom of action with activity and strength. Chest deep and broad, but not broad enough to interfere with the free play of the shoulders. *Defects*—Straight, upright shoulders. Chest dispro-

short, set on high or with a tendency to rise above the point of origin.

Body: *Neck and Throat*—Neck rising free and light from the shoulders strong in substance yet not loaded, of medium length. The throat clean and free from folds of skin; a slight wrinkle below the angle of the jaw, however, may be allowable. *Defects*—A thick, short, cloddy neck carried on a line with the top of the shoulders. Throat showing dewlap and folds of skin to a degree termed "throatiness."

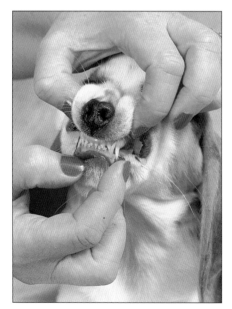

The bite of a puppy should be fairly even, as a level jaw is required in adulthood.

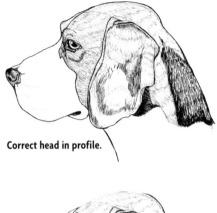

Correct head in profile.

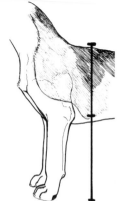

Incorrect; muzzle too snipy.

Correct forequarters; forelegs straight and in proportion to body.

Incorrect forequarters; lack of depth of chest.

Correct topline and tuck-up.

portionately wide or with lack of depth.

Back, Loin and Ribs: Back short, muscular and strong. Loin broad and slightly arched, and the ribs well sprung, giving abundance of lung room. *Defects*—Very long or swayed or roached back. Flat, narrow loin. Flat ribs.

Forelegs and Feet: *Forelegs*— Straight, with plenty of bone in proportion to size of the hound. Pasterns short and straight. *Feet*— Close, round and firm. Pad full

Incorrect; swayed back and excessive tuck-up.

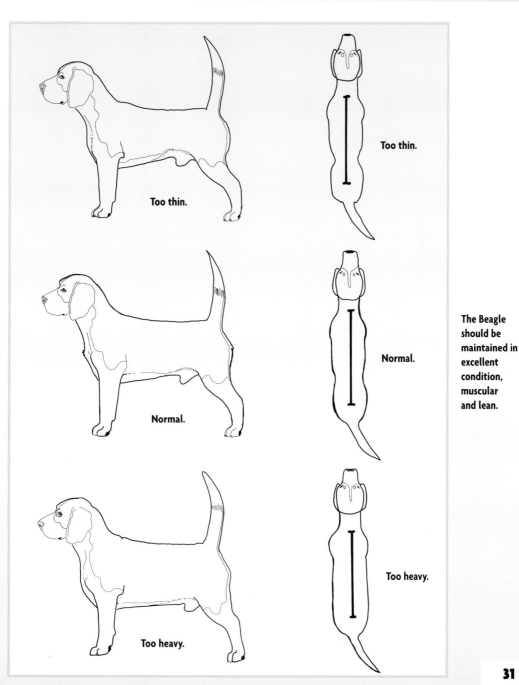

Too thin.

Too thin.

Normal.

Normal.

Too heavy.

Too heavy.

The Beagle should be maintained in excellent condition, muscular and lean.

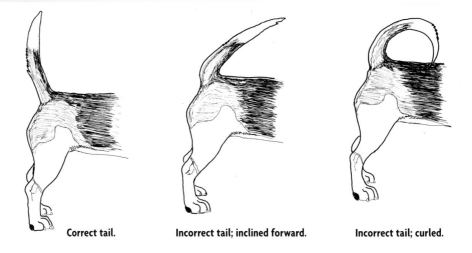

Correct tail.   Incorrect tail; inclined forward.   Incorrect tail; curled.

and hard. *Defects*—Out at elbows. Knees knuckled over forward, or bent backward. Forelegs crooked or Dachshundlike. Feet long, open or spreading.

Hips, Thighs, Hind Legs and Feet: Hips and thighs strong and well muscled, giving abundance of propelling power. Stifles strong and well let down. Hocks firm, symmetrical and moderately bent. Feet close and firm. *Defects*—Cowhocks, or straight hocks. Lack of muscle and propelling power. Open feet.

Tail: Set moderately high; carried gaily, but not turned forward over the back; with slight curve; short as compared with size of the hound; with brush. *Defects*—A long tail. Teapot curve or inclined forward from the root. Rat tail with absence of brush.

Coat: A close, hard, hound coat of medium length. *Defects*—A short, thin coat, or of a soft quality.

Color: Any true hound color.

General Appearance: A miniature Foxhound, solid and big for his inches, with the wear-and-tear look of the hound that can last in the chase and follow his quarry to the death.

Varieties: There shall be two varieties: Thirteen Inch—which shall be for hounds not exceeding 13 inches in height. Fifteen Inch—which shall be for hounds over 13 but not exceeding 15 inches in height.

Disqualification: Any hound measuring more than 15 inches shall be disqualified.

The Beagle is a miniature Foxhound, with an unmistakable expression that is gentle and pleading.

Have you ever been to the home of a friend or relative who owned an unruly dog? This untrained, attention-starved creature hurls itself at company, climbing upon your lap, mounting your leg and the like... Of course, the owner does not seem to notice or know how to discipline or control the

Selecting the Beagle puppy that best suits you will be a carefully considered but fun decision. How will you choose?

animal. A nuisance? You bet! No one wants to own a dog like that or be around one.

The Beagle is a merry little hound with boundless energy and undying enthusiasm for life. He is a bright dog who can be mischievous and adventuresome. He requires a great deal of your time from purchase throughout his puppyhood into his adolescent days, until he reaches maturity

and becomes a responsible canine citizen. Do you have the time for the most basic of daily care, a walk, no matter the weather? Your Beagle will require a degree of commitment and care all of his life, which can possibly be as long as 12 to 15 years. Are you ready to devote the time your Beagle will need and deserves? If you don't have the time, or the willingness to make time, then please don't choose a Beagle as a companion.

Space is another important consideration. The Beagle in early puppyhood may be well accommodated in a corner of your kitchen, but, after only a few months, a larger space will be required. Beagles are pack animals and, therefore, live to be a part of your pack—not apart from your pack. He wants to live in the home with the family. And outdoors, a yard with a fence is a basic and reasonable expectation.

In addition, there are the usual problems associated with puppies of any breed, such as the damages likely to be sustained by your floors, furniture, flowers, etc. Not least of all, there will be restrictions to your freedom (of movement) when planning a vacation or weekend trips. This union is a serious affair and should be deeply considered. However, once you decide, a Beagle can be the most rewarding of all breeds. A few suggestions will help in the purchase of your dog.

BUYING THE BEAGLE PUPPY

Most likely you are seeking a pet Beagle, not necessarily a show dog. This does not mean that you are looking for a second-rate model. A "pet-quality" Beagle is not like a used car or a slightly irregular suit jacket. Your pet must be as sound, healthy and temperamentally fit as any top show dog. Quality breeders treat all the pups in their litters alike. They do not attend to the potential show pups and ignore the pet pups. All pups are reared with the same care and affection.

Pet owners want a Beagle who can run smoothly and easily, who is trustworthy and reliable around children and strangers and who looks like a Beagle. Even though the owner may not be gaiting and posing his pet in front of a show judge, soundness is still important. You are not buying a black-and-tan toy dog or a shaggy, leggy greyhound, you want a Beagle—a handsome hound with a lovely head and melting, devoted expression, who is soundly built with good eyes and a loveable personality. If these qualities are not

ARE YOU PREPARED?

Unfortunately, when a puppy is bought by someone who does not take into consideration the time and attention that dog ownership requires, it is the puppy who suffers when he is either abandoned or placed in a shelter by a frustrated owner. So all of the "homework" you do in preparation for your pup's arrival will benefit you both. The more informed you are, the more you will know what to expect and the better equipped you will be to handle the ups and downs of raising a puppy. Hopefully, everyone in the household is willing to do his part in raising and caring for the pup. The anticipation of owning a dog often brings a lot of promises from excited family members: "I will walk him every day," "I will feed him," "I will house-train him," etc., but these things take time and effort, and promises can easily be forgotten as time passes, once the novelty of the new pet has worn off.

You should observe the litter to get to know each pup's individual temperament. Remember that once you bring the pup home, you will have a lot to do with shaping his personality since you are his role model.

35

important to you as a Beagle owner, then why did you choose the Beagle?

The safest method of obtaining your new Beagle puppy is to seek out a reputable breeder. This is strongly recommended whether you are looking for a pet dog or a show-quality specimen. The novice breeders and pet owners who advertise at attractive prices in the local newspapers are probably kind enough towards their dogs, but do not have the expertise or facilities required to successfully raise these animals. These pet puppies are frequently badly weaned and left with their mothers too long, failing to receive the additional nutrition of a good puppy diet. This lack of proper feeding can cause indigestion, rickets, weak bones, poor

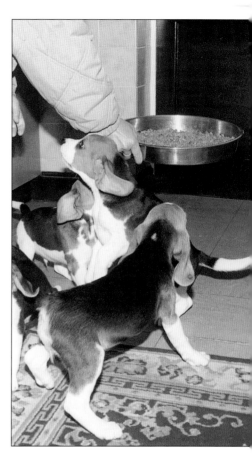

TEMPERAMENT COUNTS

Your selection of a good puppy can be determined by your needs. A show potential, a hunting companion or a good pet? It is your choice. Every puppy, however, should be of good temperament. Although show-quality puppies are bred and raised with emphasis on physical conformation, responsible breeders strive for equally good temperament. Do not buy from a breeder who concentrates solely on physical beauty at the expense of personality.

teeth and other problems. Veterinary bills may soon distort initial savings into financial or, worse, emotional loss.

Inquire about inoculations and when the puppy was last dosed for worms. How healthy and clean does the Beagle puppy appear? Check the ears for any signs of mites or irritation. Are the eyes clear and free of any debris? Look for expression in your puppy's eyes, as this is a good sign of harmony and intelligence. The look of the Beagle is always soft, wise, adoring and pleading. The puppy coat is softer than the adult coat, and should look shiny and healthy.

Note the way your choice moves. The Beagle, even in puppyhood, should show sound, deliberate movement with no tendency to stumble or drag his hind feet. Do not mistake a little puppy awkwardness for a physical defect. Look at the mouth to make sure that the bite is fairly even, although maturity can often correct minor errors present at puppyhood. If you have any doubts, ask to see the parents' mouths. This brings up an important point—do not purchase a puppy without first seeing at least one of the parents. The sire and dam of your chosen puppy will reveal much about what your Beagle will look like (and even act like) upon reaching maturity.

COMMITMENT OF OWNERSHIP
After considering all of these factors, you have most likely already made some very important decisions about selecting your puppy. You have chosen the Beagle, which means that you have decided which characteristics you want in a dog and what type of dog will best fit into your family and lifestyle. If you have selected a breeder, you have gone a step further—you

PUPPY APPEARANCE

Your puppy should have a well-fed appearance but not a distended abdomen, which may indicate worms or incorrect feeding, or both. The body should be firm, with a solid feel. The skin of the abdomen should be pale pink and clean, without signs of scratching or rash; there should be no bald patches of coat. Check the hind legs to make certain that dewclaws were removed, if any were present at birth.

have done your research and found a responsible, conscientious person who breeds sound, healthy, friendly Beagles and who should become a reliable source of help as you and your puppy adjust to life together. If you have observed a litter in action, you have obtained a firsthand look at the dynamics of a puppy "pack" and, thus, you should have learned about each pup's individual personality—perhaps you have even found one that particularly appeals to you.

However, even if you have not yet found the Beagle puppy of your dreams, observing pups will help you learn to recognize certain behavior and to determine what a pup's behavior indicates about his temperament. You will be able to pick out which pups are the leaders, which ones are less outgoing, which ones are confident, which ones are shy, playful, friendly, aggressive, etc. Equally as important, you will learn to recognize what a healthy pup should look and act like. All of these things will help you in your search, and when you find the Beagle that was meant for you, you will know it!

Researching your breed, selecting a responsible breeder and observing as many pups as possible are all important steps on the way to dog ownership. It may seem like a lot of effort...and you have not even brought the pup home yet! Remember, though, you cannot be too careful when it comes to deciding on the type of dog you want and finding out about your prospective pup's background. Buying a puppy is not—or should not be—just another whimsical purchase. This is one instance in which you

PUPPY'S PAPERS

Too often new owners are confused between the pedigree and the registration certificate. Your puppy's pedigree, essentially a family tree, is a written record of a dog's genealogy of three generations or more. The pedigree will show you the names as well as performance titles of all the dogs in your pup's background. Your breeder must provide you with a registration application, with his part properly filled out. You must complete the application and send it to the AKC with the proper fee. Every puppy must come from a litter that has been AKC-registered by the breeder, born in the USA and from a sire and dam that are also registered with the AKC.

The seller must provide you with complete records to identify the puppy. The AKC requires that the seller provide the buyer with the following: breed; sex, color and markings; date of birth; litter number (when available); names and registration numbers of the parents; breeder's name; and date sold or delivered.

actually do get to choose your own family! You may be thinking that buying a puppy should be fun—it should not be so serious and so much work. You will come to realize that, while buying a puppy is a pleasurable and exciting endeavor, it is not something to be taken lightly. Relax…the fun will start when the pup comes home!

PREPARING PUPPY'S PLACE IN YOUR HOME

Researching your breed and finding a breeder are only two aspects of the "homework" you will have to do before bringing your Beagle puppy home. You will also have to prepare your home and family for the new addition. Much as you would prepare a nursery for a newborn baby, you will need to designate a place in your home that will be the puppy's own. How you prepare your home will depend on how much freedom the dog

will be allowed. Whatever you decide, you must ensure that he has a place that he can "call his own."

When you bring your new puppy into your home, you are bringing him into what will become his home as well. Obviously, you did not buy a puppy so that he could take control of your house, but in order for a puppy to grow into a stable, well-adjusted dog, he has to feel comfortable in his surroundings. Remember, he is leaving the warmth and security of his mother and littermates, as well as the familiarity of the only place he has ever known, so it is important to make his transition as easy as possible. By preparing a place in your home for the puppy, you are making him feel as welcome as possible in a strange new place. It should not take him

If possible, insist upon seeing the dam with her pups. The pups usually turn out with a temperament like the dam's, providing you supply a loving environment and make the pup part of your "pack."

TIME TO GO HOME

Breeders rarely release puppies until they are eight to ten weeks of age. This is an acceptable age for most breeds of dog, excepting toy breeds, which are not released until around 12 weeks, given their petite sizes. If a breeder has a puppy that is 12 weeks of age or older, it is likely well socialized and house-trained. Be sure that it is otherwise healthy before deciding to take it home.

feeling. It is up to you to reassure him and to let him know, "Little guy or gal, you are going to like it here!"

WHAT YOU SHOULD BUY

CRATE
Nothing is more important to your life with your Beagle than his crate! To someone unfamiliar with the use of crates in dog training, it may seem like punishment to shut a dog in a crate, but this is not the case at all. Most breeders and trainers recommend the crate as a preferred tool for pet puppies as well as show puppies. For Beagles, the crate is key to housebreaking, an exercise that

YOUR SCHEDULE...

If you lead an erratic, unpredictable life, with daily or weekly changes in your work requirements, consider the problems of owning a puppy. The new puppy has to be fed regularly, socialized (loved, petted, handled, introduced to other people) and, most importantly, allowed to go outdoors for house-training. As the dog gets older, it can be more tolerant of deviations in its feeding and relief schedule.

long to get used to it, but the sudden shock of being transplanted is somewhat traumatic for a young pup. Imagine how a small child would feel in the same situation—that is how your puppy must be

Surely you must not tolerate a Beagle puppy that chews on your rug! Keep valuables away from the grip of growing Beagle teeth!

many Beagles and their owners find challenging.

So, to be sure, crates are not cruel—crates have many humane and highly effective uses in dog care and training. In addition to housebreaking, for example, a crate can keep your dog safe during travel. Perhaps most importantly, a crate provides your dog with a place of his own in your home. It serves as a "doggie bedroom" of sorts—your Beagle can curl up in his crate when he wants to sleep or when he just needs a break. Many dogs sleep in their crates overnight. When lined with soft bedding and with a favorite toy placed inside, a crate becomes a cozy pseudo-den for your dog. If introduced to the crate at a young age, Beagles

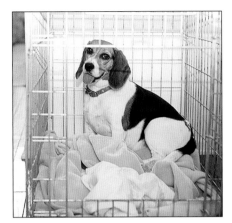

A Beagle usually loves his crate. Wire crates are the best for use inside the home so the Beagle has good ventilation and can see what's going on around him.

welcome the crate as their own special place. Although Beagles were kept in packs for generations, and therefore were not exposed to crates, *per se*, these smart hounds can be trained to become clean little dogs with a bit of patience and persistence.

As far as purchasing a crate, the type that you buy is up to you. It will most likely be one of the two most popular types: wire or fiberglass. There are advantages and disadvantages to each type. For example, a wire crate is more open, allowing the air to flow through and affording the dog a view of what is going on around him, while a fiberglass crate is sturdier. Both can double as travel crates, providing protection for the dog.

The size of the crate is another thing to consider. Puppies do not stay puppies forever—in fact, sometimes it seems as if they grow right before your eyes. A

PET INSURANCE

Investigate a pet insurance policy by talking to your vet. Depending on the age of your dog, the breed and the kind of coverage you desire, your policy can be very affordable. Most policies cover accidental injuries, poisoning, and thousands of medical problems and illnesses, including cancers. Some carriers also offer routine care and immunization coverage, including spaying/neutering, health screening and more. These policies are more costly than the others, but may be well worth the investment.

41

PHOTO COURTESY OF DOSKOCIL.

BEDDING

A soft crate pad in the dog's crate will help the dog feel more at home, and you may also like to give him a small blanket. Until you take your pup home, he has been sleeping amid the warmth of his mother and littermates, and while a blanket is not the same as a warm, breathing body, it still provides heat and something with which to snuggle. You will want to wash your pup's bedding frequently in case he has an accident in his crate, and replace or remove any padding or blanket that becomes ragged and starts to fall apart.

Believe it or not, potty accidents in the crate during puppyhood will occur less

THE RIDE HOME

Taking your dog from the breeder to your home in a car can be a very uncomfortable experience for both of you. The puppy will have been taken from his warm, friendly, safe environment and brought into a strange new environment—an environment that moves! A passenger can hold the puppy on his lap. Be prepared for loose bowels, urination, crying, whining and even fear biting. With proper love and encouragement when you arrive home, the stress of the trip should quickly disappear.

Top breeders are convinced that crate training is the best way to train a dog. Your local pet shop will offer a variety of sizes, styles and colors.

small crate may be fine for a very young Beagle pup, but it will not do him much good for long! It is best to get one that will accommodate your dog both as a pup and at full size. A medium-size crate will be necessary for a full-grown Beagle, who stands 10–16 inches high.

PUPPY PROBLEMS

The majority of problems that are commonly seen in young pups will disappear as your dog gets older. However, how you deal with problems when he is young will determine how he reacts to discipline as an adult dog. It is important to establish who is boss (it should be you!) right away when you are first bonding with your dog. This bond will set the tone for the rest of your life together, which hopefully will be a long, happy and rewarding one!

frequently than you might expect. No dog intentionally soils the area in which he sleeps…but accidents do happen, especially for the growing Beagle puppy.

Toys

Toys are a must for dogs of all ages, especially for curious playful pups. Puppies are the "children" of the dog world, and what child does not love toys? Chew toys provide enjoyment to both dog and owner—your dog will enjoy playing with his favorite toys, while you will enjoy the fact that they distract him from your expensive shoes and leather couch. Puppies love to chew; in fact, chewing is a physical need for pups as they are teething, and everything looks appetizing! The full range of your possessions—from old dish rag to

Oriental rug—are fair game in the eyes of a teething pup. Puppies are not all that discerning when it comes to finding something to literally "sink their teeth into"—everything tastes great!

Beagle puppies can be fairly aggressive chewers and only the most durable toys should be offered to them. Nylon bones are the strongest and safest to offer to your Beagle. Breeders advise owners to resist stuffed toys, because they can become de-stuffed in no time. The overly excited pup may ingest the stuffing, which is neither nutritious nor digestible.

Similarly, squeaky toys are quite popular, but must be avoided for the Beagle. Perhaps a squeaky toy can be used as an aid

Pet shops sell many products that new dog owners will need. Make your selections carefully.

43

Make sure your Beagle's crate is comfortable. Let him choose a favorite toy and put in a crate pad to make it cozy.

potentially dangerous.

Be careful of natural bones, which have a tendency to splinter into sharp, dangerous pieces. Also be careful of rawhide, which can turn into pieces that are easy to swallow or a mushy mess on your carpet. Best are the flavored bones made of materials meant for hours of chewing and that do not break off into dangerous small pieces. These come in variety of flavors that appeal to dogs: liver, chicken, bacon, etc.

Stuffed toys made for children are prohibited as the dog will certainly tear them apart and perhaps ingest a piece that could choke him.

in training, but not for free play. If a pup "disembowels" one of these, the small plastic squeaker inside can be dangerous if swallowed. Monitor the condition of all your pup's toys carefully and get rid of any that have been chewed to the point of becoming

CRATE TRAINING

During crate training, you should partition off the section of the crate in which the pup stays. If he is given too big an area, this will hinder your training efforts. Crate training is based on the fact that a dog does not like to soil his sleeping quarters, so it is ineffective to keep a pup in an area that is so big that he can eliminate in one end and get far enough away from it to sleep. Also, you want to make the crate den-like for the pup. Blankets and a favorite toy will make the crate cozy for the small pup; as he grows, you may want to evict some of his "roommates" to make more room. It will take some coaxing at first, but be patient. Given some time to get used to it, your pup will adapt to his new home-within-a-home quite nicely. Your dog will enjoy having a place of his own and you will have a place to keep your dog safe.

COLLAR

Your pup should get used to wearing a collar all the time since you will want to attach his ID tags to his collar. Also, the leash and collar go hand in hand—you have to attach the leash to something! A lightweight nylon collar will be a good choice; make sure that it fits snugly enough so that the pup cannot wriggle out of it, but loose enough so that it will not be uncomfortably tight around the pup's neck. You should be able to fit a finger in between the pup and the collar. It may take some time for your pup to get used to wearing the collar, but soon he will not even notice that it is there. Choke collars are made for training, but should only be used by an owner who knows exactly how to use it.

LEASH

A nylon leash is probably the best option as it is the most resistant to puppy teeth should your pup take a liking to chewing on his leash. Of course, this is a habit that should be nipped in the bud, but if your pup likes to chew on his leash, he has a very slim chance of being able to chew through the strong nylon. Nylon leashes are also lightweight, which is good for a young Beagle who is just getting used to the idea of walking on a leash. For everyday walking and safety purposes, the nylon leash is a good choice. As your

TOYS, TOYS, TOYS!

With a big variety of dog toys available, and so many that look like they would be a lot of fun for a dog, be careful in your selection. It is amazing what a set of puppy teeth can do to an innocent-looking toy; so, obviously, safety is a major consideration. Be sure to choose the most durable products that you can find. Hard nylon bones and toys are a safe bet, and many of them are offered in different scents and flavors that will be sure to capture your dog's attention. It is always fun to play a game of fetch with your dog, and there are balls and flying discs that are specially made to withstand dog teeth.

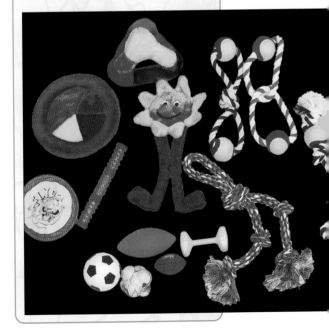

FOOD AND WATER BOWLS

Your pup will need three bowls, one for food and two for water. One water bowl should be kept inside the house and the other water bowl outside. Stainless steel or sturdy plastic bowls are popular choices. Plastic bowls are

Beagles are enthusiastic chewers and can devour cooked bones in short order. Hard nylon bones are better as they will not splinter.

pup grows up and gets used to walking on the leash, and can do it politely, you may want to purchase a flexible leash. This convenient device allows you either to extend the length to give the dog a broader area to explore or to pull in the leash when you want to keep him close.

Your Beagle should be trained to sit while you put on his collar. Accustom him to this routine while he's still a pup.

STRESS-FREE

Some experts in canine health advise that stress during a dog's early years of development can compromise and weaken his immune system, and may trigger the potential for a shortened life. They emphasize the need for happy and stress-free growing-up years.

The **BUCKLE COLLAR** is the standard collar used for everyday purposes. Be sure that you adjust the buckle on growing puppies. Check it every day. It can become too tight overnight! These collars can be made of leather or nylon. Attach your dog's identification tags to this collar.

The **CHOKE CHAIN** is made for training. It is constructed of highly polished steel so that it slides easily through the stainless steel loop. The idea is that the dog controls the pressure around his neck and he will stop pulling if the collar becomes uncomfortable. *Never* leave a choke collar on your dog when not training.

The **HALTER** is for a trained dog that has to be restrained to prevent running away, chasing a cat and the like. Considered the most humane of all collars, it is frequently used on smaller dogs on which collars are not comfortable.

47

For the show ring, a light collar/leash made from cloth or nylon is all that is necessary. But for an everyday "let's-go-for-a-walk" collar and leash, something more substantial is necessary.

Be sure to buy a high-quality collar that can be adjusted as the Beagle puppy grows.

SKULL & CROSSBONES

Thoroughly puppy-proof your house before bringing your puppy home. Never use cockroach or rodent poisons or plant fertilizers in any area accessible to the puppy. Avoid the use of toilet cleaners. Most dogs are born with "toilet-bowl sonar" and will take a drink if the lid is left open. Also keep the trash secured and out of reach.

more apt to be chewed by a Beagle, so the stainless steel type is preferable. Dogs tend not to chew on the steel variety, and these bowls can also be sterilized. Be sure to clean the dog's bowls daily.

CLEANING SUPPLIES

Until a pup is house-trained, you will be doing a lot of cleaning. "Accidents" will occur, which is okay in the beginning because the puppy does not know any better. All you can do is be prepared to clean up any accidents. Old rags, paper towels, newspapers and a safe disinfectant are good to have on hand.

PUPPY-PROOFING YOUR HOME

Aside from making sure that your Beagle will be comfortable in your home, you also have to make sure that your home is safe for your Beagle. This means taking precautions that your pup will not get into anything he should not get into and that there is nothing within his reach that may harm him should he sniff it, chew it,

Most trainers recommend using a lightweight nylon leash for your Beagle. Pet shops offer dozens of choices of collars and leashes, in different styles, colors and lengths.

Responsible law-abiding dog owners pick up their dogs' droppings wherever they occur. Pooper-scooper devices make the job quick and easy.

Stainless steel or heavy plastic bowls are sold at pet shops.

49

Provide your Beagle with durable food and water bowls that can be cleaned easily.

PHOTO COURTESY OF MIKKI PET PRODUCTS.

inspect it, etc. This probably seems obvious since, while you are primarily concerned with your pup's safety, at the same time you do not want your belongings to be ruined.

Breakables should be placed out of reach if your dog is to have full run of the house. If he is to be limited to certain places within the house, keep any potentially dangerous items in the "off-limits" areas. An electrical cord can pose a danger should the puppy decide to taste it—and who is going to convince a pup that it would not make a great chew toy? Cords should be fastened tightly against the wall. If your dog is going to spend time in a crate, make sure that there is nothing near his crate that he can reach if he sticks his curious little nose or paws through the openings. Just as you would with a child, keep

TOXIC PLANTS

Many plants can be toxic to dogs. If you see your dog carrying a piece of vegetation in his mouth, approach him in a quiet, disinterested manner, avoid eye contact, pet him and gradually remove the plant from his mouth. Alternatively, offer him a treat and maybe he'll drop the plant on his own accord. Be sure no toxic plants are growing in your yard; remember that some houseplants can be dangerous as well.

all household cleaners and chemicals where the pup cannot get to them.

It is also important to make sure that the outside of your home is safe. Of course your puppy should never be unsupervised, but a pup let loose in the yard will want to run and explore, and he should be granted that freedom. Do not let a fence give you a false sense of security; you would be surprised how crafty (and persistent) a dog can be in working out how to dig under and squeeze his way through small holes, or to jump or climb over a fence. The remedy is to make the fence high enough so that it really is impossible for your dog to get over it (about 5 feet should suffice), and well embedded into the ground. Be sure to repair or secure any gaps in the fence. Check the fence periodically to ensure that it is in good shape and make repairs as needed; a very determined pup may return to the same spot to "work on it" until he is able to get through.

THE FIRST VISIT TO THE VET
Before you bring your new Beagle home, be certain that you make an appointment with your chosen veterinarian. Although breeders will stand behind the health of their dogs, they often will not provide a health guarantee. It is advisable to have the pup's condition and health assessed by

Puppy-proofing your Beagle's outside environment means being sure your yard is well fenced and safe from pesticides, herbicides and fertilizers. Beagles, like other dogs, often lick or eat grass.

a professional before you take him home. The pup's first visit will consist of an overall examination to make sure that the pup does not have any problems that are not apparent to you. The veterinarian will also set up a schedule for the pup's vaccinations; the breeder will inform you of which

CHEMICAL TOXINS

Scour your garage for potential puppy dangers. Remove weed killers, pesticides and antifreeze materials. Antifreeze is highly toxic and just a few drops can kill a puppy or an adult dog. The sweet taste attracts the animal, who will quickly consume it from the floor or pavement.

The whole family (and your neighbors, too) should meet your new Beagle, making introductions careful and low-key. Letting the dog sniff a hand before offering a new toy is a good start.

ones the pup has already received and the vet can continue from there.

MEETING YOUR FAMILY

Everyone in the house will be excited about the puppy's coming home and will want to pet him and play with him, but it is best to make the introductions low-key so as not to overwhelm the puppy. He is apprehensive already. It is the first time he has been separated from his mother and the breeder, and the ride to your home is likely the first time he has been in a car. The last thing you want to do is smother him, as this will only frighten him further. This is not to say that human contact is not extremely necessary at this stage, because this is the time when a connection between the pup and his human family is formed. Gentle petting and soothing words should help console him, as well as just putting him down and letting him explore on his own (under your

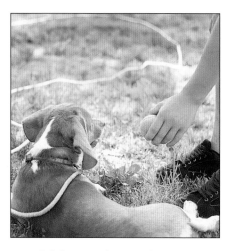

watchful eye, of course).

The pup may approach the family members or may busy himself with exploring for a while. Gradually, each person should spend some time with the pup, one at a time, crouching down to get as close to the pup's level as possible, letting him sniff their hands and petting him gently. He definitely needs human attention and he needs to be touched—this is how to form an immediate bond. Just remember that the pup is experiencing a lot of things for the first time, at the same time. There are new people, new noises, new smells and new things to investigate, so be gentle, be affectionate and be as comforting as you can be.

PUP'S FIRST NIGHT HOME

You have driven home with your new charge safely in his crate. He has been to the vet for a thorough

IN DUE TIME

It will take at least two weeks for your puppy to become accustomed to his new surroundings. Give him lots of love, attention, handling, frequent opportunities to relieve himself, a diet he likes to eat and a place he can call his own.

check-up, he has been weighed, his papers examined; perhaps he has been vaccinated and wormed as well. He has met the family and licked the whole family, including the excited children and the less-than-happy cat. He has explored his crate, his new bed, the yard and anywhere else he has been permitted. He has eaten his first meal at home and relieved himself in the proper place. He has heard lots of new sounds, smelled new friends and seen more of the outside world than ever before.

That was just the first day! He is exhausted and is ready for bed...or so you think!

It is puppy's first night and you are ready to say "Good night." Keep in mind that this is puppy's first night ever to be sleeping alone. His dam and littermates are no longer at paw's length and he is a bit scared, cold and lonely. Be reassuring to your new family

NATURAL TOXINS

Examine your lawn and home landscaping before bringing your puppy home. Many varieties of plants have leaves, stems or flowers that are toxic if ingested, and you can depend on a curious puppy to investigate them. Ask your vet for information on poisonous plants or research them at your library. Remove any potentially dangerous plants from your yard and garden.

member, but this is not the time to spoil him and give in to his inevitable whining.

Puppies whine to let others know where they are and hopefully to get company out of it. At bedtime, place your pup in his crate in his room and close the crate door. Mercifully, he will fall asleep without a peep. When the inevitable occurs, ignore the whining; he is fine. Be strong and keep his interests in mind. Do not allow your heart to become guilty and visit the pup. He will eventually fall asleep.

Many breeders recommend placing a piece of bedding from his former home in his new bed so that he recognizes the scent of his littermates. Others like to fill an old sock with other old socks, making a puppy-like lump for the puppy to snuggle with. Others still advise placing a hot water bottle in his bed for warmth. This

A secure fence should keep the Beagle safely confined in your yard, but your dog should never be left outdoors unsupervised.

latter may be a good idea provided the pup does not attempt to suckle—he will get good and wet and may not fall asleep so fast.

Puppy's first night can be somewhat stressful for the pup and his new family. Remember that you are setting the tone of nighttime at your house. Unless you want to play with your pup every night at 10 p.m., midnight and 2 a.m., do not initiate the habit. Your family will thank you, and, in time, so will your pup!

PREVENTING PUPPY PROBLEMS

Socialization

Now that you have done all of the preparatory work and have helped your pup get accustomed to his new home and family, it is about time for you to have some fun! Socializing your Beagle pup gives you the opportunity to show off your new friend, and your pup gets to reap the benefits of being an irresistible creature that people

SOCIALIZATION

Thorough socialization includes not only meeting new people but also being introduced to new experiences such as riding in the car, having his coat brushed, hearing the television, walking in a crowd—the list is endless. The more your pup experiences, and the more positive the experiences are, the less of a shock and the less frightening it will be for your pup to encounter new things.

Proper socialization includes meeting the family cat.

will want to pet and, in general, think is absolutely precious!

Besides getting to know his new family, your puppy should be exposed to other people, animals and situations. This will help him become well adjusted as he grows up and less prone to being timid or fearful of the new things he will encounter. Of course, he should not meet other animals until his course of injections is complete.

Your pup's socialization began at the breeder's, but now it is your responsibility to continue. The socialization he receives up until the age of 12 weeks is the most critical, as this is the time when he forms his impressions of the outside world. Lack of socialization can manifest itself in fear and aggression as the dog grows up. He needs lots of human contact, affection, handling and exposure to other animals. Be careful during the eight-to-ten-week-old period, also known as the fear period. The interaction he receives during this time should be gentle and reassuring.

Once your pup has received his necessary vaccinations, feel free to take him out and about (on his leash, of course). Puppies do not have to try to make friends, and there will be no shortage of people who will want to introduce themselves. Just make sure that you carefully supervise each new encounter. If the

TRAINING TIP

Training your puppy takes much patience and can be frustrating at times, but you should see results from your efforts. If you have a puppy that seems untrainable, take him to a trainer or behaviorist. The dog may have a personality problem that requires the help of a professional, or perhaps you need help in learning how to train your dog.

neighborhood children want to say hello, for example, that is great. Children and pups most often make great companions. However, be wary of any excited children who might unintentionally handle a pup too roughly. Likewise, an overzealous pup might playfully nip a little too hard. You want to make socialization experiences positive ones; what a pup learns during this very formative stage will impact his attitude toward future encounters. A pup that has a bad experience with a child may grow up to be a dog that is shy around or aggressive toward children, and you want your dog to be comfortable around everyone.

CONSISTENCY IN TRAINING
Beagles, being true pack animals, naturally need a leader, or else they try to establish dominance in their packs. When you bring a

55

Beagle

Beagles are pack animals. This famous painting from the turn of the twentieth century was rendered by T. Ivester Lloyd, who was not only an excellent painter but also a breeder of Beagles, a Master of the Pack and a recognized authority on hounds in general.

Beagle into your family, who becomes the leader and who becomes the "pack" is entirely up to you! Your pup's intuitive quest for dominance, coupled with the fact that it is nearly impossible to look at an adorable Beagle pup, with his "puppy-dog" eyes and too-big-for-his-head-still-floppy ears, and not cave in, give the pup an unfair advantage in getting the upper hand!

A pup will definitely test the waters to see what he can and cannot get away with. Do not give in to those pleading eyes—stand your ground when it comes to disciplining the pup and make sure that all family members do

the same. It will only confuse the pup when Mother tells him to get off the couch when he is used to sitting up there with Father to watch the nightly news. Avoid discrepancies by having all members of the household decide on the rules before the pup comes home...and be consistent in enforcing them! Early training shapes the dog's personality, so you cannot be unclear in what you expect.

COMMON PUPPY PROBLEMS

The best way to prevent puppy problems is to be proactive in stopping an undesirable behavior as soon as it starts. The old saying

"You can't teach an old dog new tricks" does not necessarily hold true, but it *is* true that it is much easier to discourage bad behavior in a young developing pup than to wait until the pup's bad behavior becomes the adult dog's bad habit. There are some problems that are especially prevalent in puppies as they develop.

NIPPING

As puppies start to teethe, they feel the need to sink their teeth into anything. Unfortunately, that includes your fingers, arms, hair, toes...whatever happens to be available. You may find this behavior cute for about the first five seconds...until you feel just how sharp those puppy teeth are. This is something you want to discourage immediately and consistently with a firm "No!" (or whatever number of firm "Nos" it takes for him to understand that you mean business) and replace your finger with an appropriate chew toy. While this behavior is merely annoying when the dog is still young, it can become dangerous as your Beagle's adult teeth grow in and his jaws develop if he thinks that it is okay to gnaw on human appendages.

WHINING/CRYING

Your pup will often cry, whine, whimper, howl or make some type of commotion when he is left alone. This is basically his way of calling out for attention to make sure that you know he is there and that you have not forgotten about him. He feels insecure when he is left alone, when you are out of the house and he is in

CHEWING TIPS

Chewing goes hand in hand with nipping in the sense that a teething puppy is always looking for a way to soothe his aching gums. In this case, instead of chewing on you, he may have taken a liking to your favorite shoe or something else which he should not be chewing. Again, realize that this is a normal canine behavior that does not need to be discouraged, only redirected. Your pup just needs to be taught what is acceptable to chew on and what is off-limits. Consistently tell him "No!" when you catch him chewing on something forbidden and give him a chew toy.

Conversely, praise him when you catch him chewing on something appropriate. In this way, you are discouraging the inappropriate behavior and reinforcing the desired behavior. The puppy's chewing should stop after his adult teeth have come in, but an adult dog continues to chew for various reasons—perhaps because he is bored, needs to relieve tension or just likes to chew. That is why it is important to redirect his chewing when he is still young.

his crate or when you are in another part of the house and he cannot see you. The noise he is making is an expression of the anxiety he feels at being alone, so he needs to be taught that being alone is okay. You are not actually training the dog to stop making noise, you are training him to feel comfortable when he is alone and thus removing the need for him to make the noise.

This is where the crate with cozy bedding and a favorite toy comes in handy. You want to know that he is safe when you are not there to supervise, and you know that he will be safe in his crate rather than roaming freely about the house. In order for the pup to stay in his crate without making a fuss, he needs to be comfortable there. On that note, it is extremely important that the crate is never used as a form of punishment, or the pup will have a negative association with the crate.

Accustom the pup to the crate in short, gradually increasing time intervals in which you put him in the crate, maybe with a treat, and stay in the room with him. If he cries or makes a fuss, do not go to him, but stay in his sight. Gradually he will realize that staying in his crate is okay without your help, and it will not be so traumatic for him when you are not around. You may want to leave the radio on softly when you leave the house; the sound of human voices may be comforting to him.

Breeders must accustom their litters to experiences beyond the whelping pen. A well-socialized puppy will adjust to life in his new home far more gracefully than puppies without exposure to people and other animals.

A Worthy Investment

Veterinary studies have proven that a balanced high-quality diet pays off in your dog's coat quality, behavior and activity level. Invest in premium brands for the maximum payoff with your dog.

WHAT TO FEED YOUR BEAGLE

What more important consideration has an owner than "what
should I feed my growing

Beagle?" This matter may appear
simple, but there are many factors
that must be considered. Today
the choices of food for your
Beagle are many and varied.
There are simply dozens of brands
of food in all sorts of flavors and
textures, ranging from puppy diets
to those for seniors. There are
even hypoallergenic and low-
calorie diets available. Because
your Beagle's food has a bearing
on coat, health and temperament,
it is essential that the most
suitable diet be selected for a
Beagle of his age. It is fair to say,
however, that even dedicated
owners can be somewhat
perplexed by the enormous range
of foods available. Only
understanding what is best for
your dog will help you reach an
informed decision.

Dog foods are produced in
three basic types: dry, semi-moist
and canned. Dry foods are useful
for the cost-conscious for overall
they tend to be less expensive
than semi-moist or canned. These
contain the least fat and the most
preservatives. In general, canned
foods are made up of 60–70%
water, while semi-moist ones
often contain so much sugar that

FOOD PREFERENCE

Selecting the best dry dog food is
difficult. There is no majority
consensus among veterinary scientists
as to the value of nutrient analysis
(protein, fat, fiber, moisture, ash,
minerals, etc.). All agree, however, that
feeding trials are what matter most,
but you also have to consider the
individual dog. The dog's weight, age
and activity level, and what pleases
his taste, all must be considered. It is
probably best to take the advice of
your veterinarian. Every dog's dietary
requirements vary, even during the
lifetime of a particular dog.

If your dog is fed a good dry food,
he does not require supplements of
meat or vegetables. "Extras" only
should be added under the vet's
advice. Dogs do appreciate a little
variety in their diets, so you may
choose to stay with the same brand
but vary the flavor. Alternatively, you
may wish to add a little flavored stock
to give a difference to the taste.

they are perhaps the least preferred by owners, even though their dogs seem to like them.

When selecting your dog's diet, three stages of development must be considered: the puppy stage, the adult stage and the senior stage.

PUPPY STAGE

Puppies instinctively want to suck milk from their mother's teats and a normal puppy will exhibit this behavior from just a few moments following birth. If puppies do not attempt to suckle within the first half-hour or so, the breeder should encourage them to do so by placing them on the nipples, having selected ones with plenty of milk. This early milk supply is important in providing colostrum to protect the puppies during the first eight to ten weeks of their lives. Although a mother's milk is much better than any milk formula, despite there being some excellent ones available, if the puppies do not feed, the breeder will have to feed them himself. For those with less experience, advice from a veterinarian is important so that not only the right quantity of milk but also that of correct quality is fed, at suitably frequent intervals, usually every two hours during the first few days of life.

Puppies should be allowed to nurse from their mothers for about the first six weeks, although from

Beagle puppies' first meals come from their dam. Puppies should be allowed to nurse from their dam for about the first six weeks of their lives.

FEEDING TIPS

Dog food must be served at room temperature, neither too hot nor too cold. Fresh water, changed often and served in a clean bowl, is mandatory, especially when feeding dry food.

Never feed your dog from the table while you are eating, and never feed your dog leftovers from your own meal. They usually contain too much fat and too much seasoning.

Dogs must chew their food. Hard pellets are excellent; soups and stews are to be avoided. Don't add leftovers or any "extras" to normal dog food. The normal food is usually balanced, and adding something extra destroys the balance.

Except for age-related changes, dogs do not require dietary variations. They can be fed the same diet, day after day, without becoming bored or ill.

61

introduce alternate milk and meat meals initially, building up to weaning time.

By the time the puppies are seven or a maximum of eight weeks old, they should be fully weaned and fed solely on a proprietary puppy food. Selection of the most suitable, good-quality diet at this time is essential, for a puppy's fastest growth rate is during the first year of life. Veterinarians are usually able to offer advice in this regard. The frequency of meals will be reduced over time and eventually you will switch your puppy to an adult food.

Puppy and junior diets should be well balanced for the needs of your dog, so that, except in certain circumstances, additional vitamins, minerals and proteins will not be required.

ADULT DIETS

A dog is considered an adult when he has stopped growing. When you switch your dog to an adult food will depend on the individual dog's development and type of food. Again you should rely upon your veterinarian, breeder or dietary specialist to recommend an acceptable maintenance diet and advise on the proper age to switch. Major dog-food manufacturers specialize in this type of food, and it is just necessary for you to select the one best suited to your dog's needs.

GRAIN-BASED DIETS

Some less expensive dog foods are based on grains and other plant proteins. While these products may appear to be attractively priced, many breeders prefer a diet based on animal proteins and believe that they are more conducive to your dog's health. Many grain-based diets rely on soy protein, which may cause flatulence (passing gas).

There are many cases, however, when your dog might require a special diet. These special requirements should only be recommended by your veterinarian.

the third or fourth week the breeder will begin to introduce small portions of suitable solid food. Most breeders like to

TEST FOR PROPER DIET

A good test for proper diet is the color, odor and firmness of your dog's stool. A healthy dog usually produces three semi-hard stools per day. The stools should have no unpleasant odor. They should be the same color from excretion to excretion. Report any changes or abnormalities to your vet.

Active dogs have different requirements than sedate dogs.

SENIOR DIETS

As dogs get older, their metabolism changes. The older dog usually exercises less, moves more slowly and sleeps more. This change in lifestyle and physiological performance requires a change in diet. Since these changes take place slowly, they might not be recognizable. What *is* easily recognizable is weight gain. By continuing to feed your dog an adult-maintenance diet when he is slowing down metabolically, your dog will gain weight. Obesity in an older dog compounds the health problems that already accompany old age.

As your dog gets older, few of his organs function up to par. The kidneys slow down and the intestines become less efficient. These age-related factors are best handled with a change in diet and a change in feeding schedule to give smaller portions that are more easily digested.

There is no single best diet for every older dog. While many dogs do well on light or senior diets, other dogs do better on puppy diets or other special premium diets such as lamb and rice. Be sensitive to your senior Beagle's diet and this will help control other problems that may arise with your old friend.

Water is just as important as food. The water bowl should be cleaned daily and the water changed several times a day.

WATER

Just as your dog needs proper nutrition from his food, water is an essential "nutrient" as well. Water keeps the dog's body properly hydrated and promotes normal function of the body's systems. During housebreaking, it is necessary to keep an eye on how much water your Beagle is drinking, but once he is reliably trained he should have access to clean fresh water at all times, especially if you feed dry food. Your Beagle should have a bowl of water available to him inside your

63

home as well as outdoors. Make sure that the dog's water bowls are clean, and change the water often. Small water bowls are made especially to attach to the crate door; these are recommended when your housebroken Beagle is left in his crate for several hours at a time, or overnight.

EXERCISE

Despite the Beagle's ancestors' running in packs on vigorous

hunts across the vast countryside, not all Beagles exhibit that "get-up-and-riot" attitude. Beagle parents may need to motivate their charges to charge (and run and play). While Beagle pups are most usually enthusiastic about exercise and play, adult Beagles may not choose to partake as readily. A sedentary lifestyle is as harmful to a dog as it is to a person, and Beagles as a breed have the propensity for obesity.

Regular walks, play sessions in the yard or letting the dog run free in the fenced yard under your supervision are sufficient forms of exercise for the Beagle. However, a Beagle puppy needs time to grow up and develop stamina before you embark on strenuous forms of exercise, long walks or even short runs. For those who are more ambitious, you will find that your adolescent or adult Beagle also enjoys an occasional hike or even a swim!

Bear in mind that an overweight dog should never be suddenly over-exercised; instead, he should be allowed to increase exercise slowly. Not only is exercise essential to keep the dog's body fit, it is essential to his mental well-being. A bored dog will find something to do, which often manifests itself in some type of destructive behavior. In this sense, exercising the dog is essential for the owner's mental well-being as well!

The minimum amount of exercise for an adult Beagle is several moderate walks each day. It will be equally good for you!

GROOMING EQUIPMENT

How much grooming equipment you purchase will depend on how much grooming you are going to do. Here are some basics:

- Natural bristle brush
- Slicker brush
- Hound glove
- Metal comb
- Scissors or shears
- Rubber mat
- Dog shampoo
- Spray hose attachment
- Towels
- Ear cleaner
- Cotton balls
- Nail clippers

GROOMING

BRUSHING

A natural bristle brush, a slicker brush or a hound glove can be used for regular routine brushing. Daily brushing is effective for removing dead hair and stimulating the dog's natural oils to add shine and a healthy look to the coat. Although the Beagle's coat is short and close, it does require a five-minute once-over to keep it looking its shiny best. Regular grooming sessions are also a good way to spend time with your dog. Many dogs grow to like the feel of being brushed and will enjoy the daily routine.

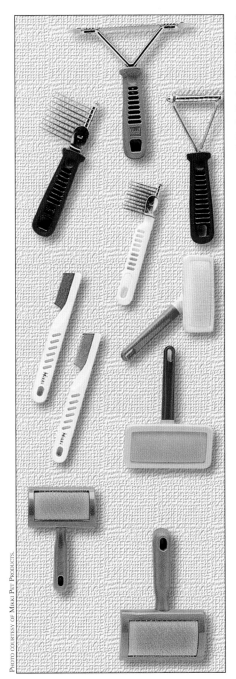

Your local pet shop will have a large supply of grooming tools from which you can select the necessary equipment for maintaining your Beagle's coat.

PHOTO COURTESY OF MIKKI PET PRODUCTS.

BATHING

Dogs do not need to be bathed as often as humans, but occasional bathing is essential for healthy skin and a clean, shiny coat. Again, like most anything, if you accustom your pup to being bathed as a puppy, it will be second nature by the time he grows up. You want your dog to be at ease in the bath or else it could end up a wet, soapy, messy ordeal for both of you!

Brush your Beagle thoroughly before wetting his coat. This will get rid of any dead hair or dust before you start. Make sure that your dog has a good non-slip surface to stand on. Begin by wetting the dog's coat. A shower or hose attachment is necessary for thoroughly wetting and rinsing the coat. Check the water temperature to make sure that it is

Top: Your Beagle should enjoy the feel of a once-over with a hound glove. Center: The hound glove is rough on one side. Below, right: The hound glove gives the coat an all-over shine.

SOAP IT UP

The use of human soap products like shampoo, bubble bath and hand soap can be damaging to a dog's coat and skin. Human products are too strong; they remove the protective oils coating the dog's hair and skin that make him water-resistant. Use only shampoo made especially for dogs. You may like to use a medicated shampoo, which will help to keep external parasites at bay.

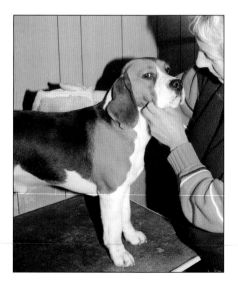

neither too hot nor too cold.

Next, apply shampoo to the dog's coat and work it into a good lather. You should purchase a shampoo that is made for dogs. Do not use a product made for human hair. Wash the head last; you do not want shampoo to drip into the dog's eyes while you are washing the rest of his body. Work the shampoo all the way down to the skin. You can use this opportunity to check the skin for any bumps, bites or other abnormalities. Do not neglect any area of the body— get all of the hard-to-reach places.

Once the dog has been thoroughly shampooed, he

requires an equally thorough rinsing. Shampoo left in the coat can be irritating to the skin. Protect his eyes from the shampoo by shielding them with your hand and directing the flow of water in the opposite direction. You should also avoid getting water in the ear canal. Be prepared for your dog to shake out his coat— you might want to stand back, but

Make sure the water you use when bathing your Beagle is neither too hot nor too cold.

Keep the water spray away from the Beagle puppy's face.

make sure you have a hold on the dog to keep him from running through the house.

EAR CLEANING
The ears should be kept clean and any excess hair inside the ear should be carefully plucked. Ears

After the bath, dry your Beagle before you let him loose, or else he'll shake and give you a shower in return.

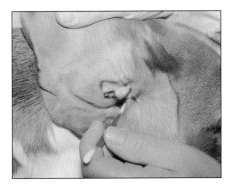

Do not probe into your Beagle's ear. It is much safer to use a cotton ball and to clean only that which you can see.

67

Carefully remove dirt and debris around the eyes with a very soft wipe.

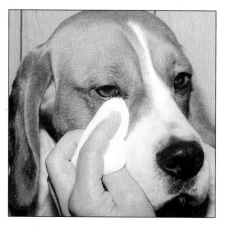

Opposite page: Dog hairs, which appear healthy. The cuticle (outer covering of the hair) is uniform with just a little dandruff. Enlargement is 250 times actual size.

can be cleaned with a cotton ball and special cleaner or ear powder made especially for dogs. Be on the lookout for any signs of infection or ear-mite infestation. If

Your local pet shop should have special canine nail clippers.

BATHING BEAUTY

Once you are sure that the dog is thoroughly rinsed, squeeze the excess water out of his coat with your hand and dry him with a heavy towel. You may choose to use a blow dryer on his coat or just let it dry naturally. In cold weather, never allow your dog outside with a wet coat.

There are "dry bath" products on the market, which are sprays and powders intended for spot cleaning, that can be used between regular baths if necessary. They are not substitutes for regular baths, but they are easy to use for touch-ups as they do not require rinsing. They are usually applied to the coat and brushed out.

your Beagle has been shaking his head or scratching at his ears frequently, this usually indicates a problem. If his ears have an unusual odor, this is a sure sign of mite infestation or infection, and a signal to have his ears checked by the veterinarian.

NAIL CLIPPING

Your Beagle should be accustomed to having his nails trimmed at an early age, since it will be part of your maintenance routine throughout his life. Not only does it look nicer, but long nails can be sharp if they scratch someone unintentionally. Also, a long nail has a better chance of ripping and bleeding, or causing the feet to spread. If you can hear your dog's nails' clicking on the floor when he walks, his nails are too long.

Before you start cutting, make

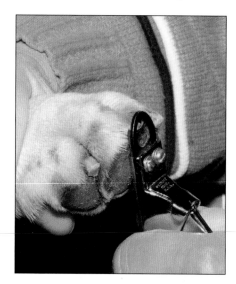

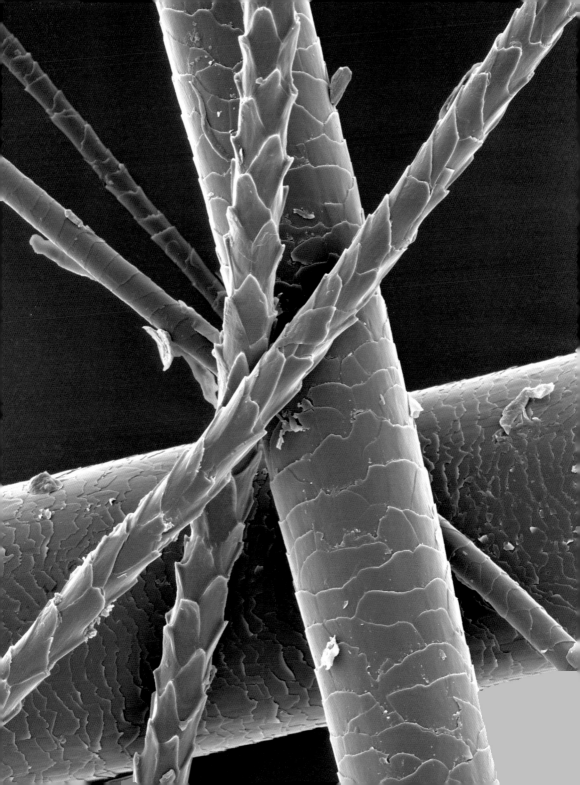

Nail Maintenance

Quick

Nail Casing

Cut Line

Dark-Colored Nails

With black or dark nails, where the quick is not easy to see, it's best to clip only the tip of the nail or to use a file.

Light-Colored Nails

In light-colored nails, clipping is much simpler because you can see the vein (or quick) that grows inside the casing.

EXERCISE ALERT!

You should be careful where you exercise your dog. Many countryside areas have been sprayed with chemicals that are highly toxic to both dogs and humans. Never allow your dog to eat grass or drink from puddles on either public or private grounds, as the run-off water may contain chemicals from sprays and herbicides. For long walks or on hot days, bring along some water from home for your dog.

sure you can identify the "quick" in each nail. The quick is a blood vessel that runs through the center of each nail and grows rather close to the end. It will bleed if accidentally cut, which will be quite painful for the dog as it contains nerve endings. Keep some type of clotting agent on hand, such as a styptic pencil or styptic powder (the type used for shaving). This will stop the bleeding quickly when applied to the end of the cut nail. Do not panic if you cut the quick, just

PEDICURE TIPS

A dog that spends a lot of time outside on a hard surface, such as cement or pavement, will have his nails naturally worn down and may not need to have them trimmed as often, except maybe in the colder months when he is not outside as much. Regardless, it is best to get your dog accustomed to the nail-trimming procedure at an early age so that he is used to it. Some dogs are especially sensitive about having their feet touched, but if a dog has experienced it since puppyhood, it should not bother him.

You can purchase an electric tool to grind down a dog's nails rather than cut them. Some dogs don't seem to mind the electric grinder but will object strongly to nail clippers. See how your dog reacts when clipping his nails.

Check your Beagle's long ears regularly; be on the lookout for signs of infection or ear-mite infestation.

stop the bleeding and talk soothingly to your dog. Once he has calmed down, move on to the next nail. It is better to clip a little at a time, particularly with black-nailed dogs.

Hold your pup steady as you begin trimming his nails; you do not want him to make any sudden movements or run away. Talk to him soothingly and stroke him as you clip. Holding his foot in your hand, simply take off the end of each nail in one quick clip. You should purchase nail clippers that are specially made for dogs.

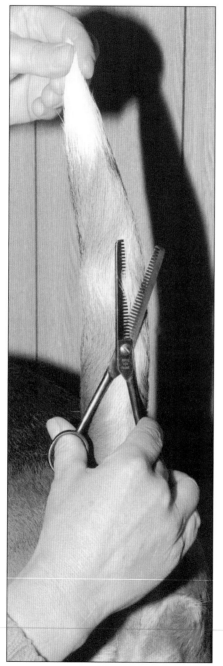

Thinning shears (shown here) are helpful in tidying up the tail.

TRAVELING WITH YOUR DOG

CAR TRAVEL

You should accustom your Beagle to riding in a car at an early age. You may or may not take him in the car often, but at the very least he will need to go to the vet and you do not want these trips to be traumatic for the dog or a big hassle for you. The safest way for a dog to ride in the car is in his crate. If he uses a crate in the house, you can use the same crate for traveling. Another option is a specially made safety harness for dogs, which straps the dog in much like a seat belt. Do not let the dog roam loose in the vehicle—this is very dangerous! If you should stop short, your dog can be thrown and injured. If the dog starts climbing on you and pestering you while you are driving, you will not be able to concentrate on the road. It is an unsafe situation for everyone—human and canine.

TRAVEL TIP

The most extensive travel you do with your dog may be limited to trips to the veterinarian's office—or you may decide to bring him along for long distances when the family goes on vacation. Whichever the case, it is important to acclimate your dog to the car and to consider his safety while traveling.

For long trips, be prepared to stop to let the dog relieve himself. Bring along whatever you need to clean up after him. You should take along some paper towels and perhaps some old bath towels for use should he have a potty accident in the car or suffer from motion sickness.

AIR TRAVEL
Contact your chosen airline before proceeding with your travel plans that include your Beagle. The dog will be required to travel in a fiberglass crate and you should always check in advance with the airline regarding specific requirements for the crate's size, type and labeling. To help put the dog at ease, give him one of his favorite toys in the crate. Do not feed the dog for several hours prior to checking in so that you minimize his need to relieve himself. However, some airlines require that the dog must be fed within four hours of arriving at the

airport, in which case a light meal is best. For long trips, you will have to attach food and water bowls to the dog's crate so that airline employees can tend to him between legs of the trip.

Make sure your dog is properly identified and that your contact information appears on

his ID tags and on his crate. Your Beagle will travel in a different area of the plane than the human passengers, so every rule must be

You should only travel with your Beagle while he is confined to his crate in the car. A dog unrestrained in the car is a danger to all concerned.

Solid, sturdy crates are used by airlines to transport pets. Make your airline travel plans well in advance if you intend to take your Beagle along.

NO PARKING

Never leave your dog alone in the car. In hot weather, your dog can die from the high temperature inside a closed vehicle; even a car parked in the shade can heat up very quickly. Leaving the window open is dangerous as well since the dog can hurt himself trying to get out.

followed to prevent the risk of getting separated from your dog.

VACATIONS AND BOARDING

So you want to take a family vacation—and you want to include *all* members of the family. You would probably make arrangements for accommodations ahead of time anyway, but this is especially important when traveling with a dog. You do not want to make an overnight stop at the only place around for miles and find out that they do not allow dogs. Also, you do not want to reserve a place for your family without confirming that you are traveling with a dog because, if it is against their policy, you may not

Given the breed's adaptability and easygoing nature, it does quite well in kennel environments. Boarding your Beagle should not present much problem for you, provided that you can locate a well-maintained kennel.

COLLAR REQUIRED

If your dog gets lost, he is not able to ask for directions home. Identification tags fastened to the collar give important information—the dog's name, the owner's name, the owner's address and a telephone number where the owner can be reached. This

makes it easy for whoever finds the dog to contact the owner and arrange to have the dog returned. An added advantage is that a person will be more likely to approach a lost dog who has ID tags on his collar; it tells the person that this is somebody's pet rather than a stray. This is the easiest and fastest method of identification, provided that the tags stay on the collar and the collar stays on the dog. This is one of the reasons for accustoming your dog to his everyday collar.

have a place to stay.

Alternatively, if you are traveling and choose not to bring your Beagle, you will have to make arrangements for him while you are away. Some

Select a boarding kennel that is convenient to your home, clean and large enough to provide your dog ample daily exercise.

LOST AND FOUND

You have a valuable dog. If the dog is lost or stolen, you would undoubtedly become extremely upset. You would hope that someone finds your Beagle and returns him to you. Likewise, if you encounter a lost dog, notify the owners, if the dog has tags, or the police or local animal shelter.

options are to take him to a neighbor's house to stay while you are gone, to have a trusted neighbor stop in often or stay at your house or to bring your dog to a reputable boarding kennel. If you choose to board him at a kennel, you should visit in advance to see the kennel, how clean it is and where the dogs are kept. Talk to some of the

Having your Beagle puppy tattooed is a permanent way to help ensure his return should he get lost or stolen.

PHOTO RETOUCHED FOR CLARITY.

IDENTIFICATION OPTIONS

As puppies become more and more expensive, especially those puppies of high quality for showing and/or breeding, they have a greater chance of being stolen. As a dog owner, you want to take every precautionary measure to ensure that your dog stays safe and with you. The usual collar dog tag is, of course, easily removed. But there are two more permanent techniques that have become widely used for identification.

The puppy microchip implantation involves the injection of a small microchip, about the size of a corn kernel, under the skin of the dog. If your dog shows up at a clinic or shelter, or is offered for resale under less-than-savory circumstances, he can be positively identified by the microchip. The microchip is scanned, and a registry quickly identifies you as the owner.

Tattooing is done on various parts of the dog, from his belly to his cheeks. The number tattooed can be your telephone number or any other number that you can easily memorize. When professional dog thieves see a tattooed dog, they usually lose interest. For the safety of our dogs, no laboratory facility or dog broker will accept a tattooed dog as stock. Both microchipping and tattooing can be done at your local veterinary clinic.

Always keep a close eye on your Beagle to keep him out of trouble. Certain shrubs, especially those with thorns or berries, can be extremely harmful to "snoopy" Beagles.

employees and see how they treat the dogs—do they spend time with the dogs, play with them, exercise them, etc.? Also find out the kennel's policy on vaccinations and what they require. This is for all of the dogs' safety, since when dogs are kept together, there is a greater risk of diseases being passed from dog to dog.

ON-LEAD ONLY

When traveling, never let your dog off-lead in a strange area. Your dog could run away out of fear, decide to chase a passing squirrel or cat or follow the trail of an enticing scent. If any of these happen, you might never see your canine friend again.

IDENTIFICATION

Your Beagle is your valued companion and friend. That is why you always keep a close eye on him and you have made sure that he cannot escape from the yard or wriggle out of his collar and run away from you. However, accidents can happen and there may come a time when your dog unexpectedly gets separated from you. If this unfortunate event should occur, the first thing on your mind will be finding him. Proper identification, including an ID tag, a tattoo and possibly a microchip, will increase the chances of his being returned to you safely and quickly. If microchipping, be sure to register your Beagle with a legitimate national registry.

77

The first thing the Beagle trainer must overcome is the Beagle's nose! This breed, like all the other scenthounds, is easily distracted by the power of its own snout!

and rhythms that set your heart singing and your body swaying.

The same is true with your Beagle. Any dog is a big responsibility and, if not trained sensibly, may develop unacceptable behavior that annoys you or could even cause family friction.

To train your Beagle, you may like to enroll in an obedience class. Teach him good manners as you learn how and why he behaves the way he does. Find out how to communicate with your dog and how to recognize and understand his communications with you. Suddenly the dog takes on a new role in your life—he is clever, interesting, well behaved and fun to be with. He demonstrates his bond of devotion to you daily. In other words, your Beagle does wonders for your

Can a Beagle be trained? Is it possible to have more success than poor ole Charlie Brown had with Snoopy? Yes, it is possible and yes, it is necessary. Living with an untrained Beagle is a lot like owning a piano that you do not know how to play—it is a nice object to look at, but it does not do much more than that to bring you pleasure. Now try taking piano lessons, and suddenly the piano comes alive and brings forth magical sounds

ATTENTION!

Your dog is actually training you at the same time you are training him. Dogs do things to get attention. They usually repeat whatever succeeds in getting your attention.

ego because he constantly reminds you that you are not only his leader, you are his hero!

Those involved with teaching dog obedience and counseling owners about their dogs' behavior have discovered some interesting facts about dog ownership. For example, training dogs when they are puppies results in the highest rate of success in developing well-mannered and well-adjusted adult dogs. Training an older dog, from six months to six years of age, can produce almost equal results, providing that the owner accepts the dog's slower rate of learning capability and is willing to work patiently to help the dog succeed at developing to his fullest potential. Unfortunately, many owners of untrained adult dogs lack the patience factor, so they do not persist until their dogs are successful at learning partic-ular behaviors.

Training a puppy aged 10 to 16 weeks (20 weeks at the most) is like working with a dry sponge in a pool of water. The pup soaks up whatever you show him and constantly looks for more things to do and learn. At this early age, his body is not yet producing hormones, and therein lies the reason for such a high rate of success. Without hormones, he is focused on his owners and not particularly

OBEDIENCE SCHOOL

Taking your dog to an obedience school may be the best investment in time and money you can ever make. You will enjoy the benefits for the lifetime of your dog and you will have the opportunity to meet people who have similar expectations for companion dogs.

All dogs respond favorably to gentle treatment. Keep this in mind when training your Beagle.

79

Don't carry your
puppy to his relief
area. Let him walk
or he will never
learn the routine of
going there
on his own.

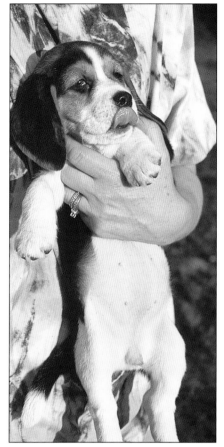

warmly, he will be happy to greet the person as well. If, however, you are hesitant or anxious about the approach of a stranger, he will respond accordingly.

Once the puppy begins to produce hormones, his natural curiosity emerges and he begins to investigate the world around him. It is at this time when you may notice that the untrained dog begins to wander away from you and even ignore your commands to stay close.

You usually will be able to find classes within a reasonable distance from your home, but you also do a lot to train your dog yourself. Sometimes there are classes available, but the tuition is too costly. Whatever the circumstances, the solution to training your dog without formal obedience lessons lies within the pages of this book.

This chapter is devoted to

interested in investigating other places, dogs, people, etc. You are his leader: his provider of food, water, shelter and security. He latches onto you and wants to stay close. He will usually follow you from room to room, will not let you out of his sight when you are outdoors with him and will respond in like manner to the people and animals you encounter. If you greet a friend

THINK BEFORE YOU BARK

Dogs are sensitive to their masters' moods and emotions. Keep this is mind and use your voice wisely when communicating with your dog. Never raise your voice at your dog unless you are angry and trying to correct him. "Barking" at your dog can become as meaningless as "dogspeak" is to you.

helping you train your Beagle at home. If the recommended procedures are followed, you may expect positive results that will prove rewarding to both you and your dog.

Whether your new charge is a puppy or a mature adult, the methods of teaching and the techniques we use in training basic behaviors are the same. After all, no dog, whether puppy or adult, likes harsh or inhumane methods. All creatures, however, respond favorably to gentle motivational methods and sincere praise and encouragement. Now let us get started.

HOUSEBREAKING

Beagles are notoriously more difficult to housebreak than other dogs. The same might be said for the other scenthound breeds (such as the Basset Hound and Foxhound). Nonethe-

Beagle puppies sometimes have "accidents" in their beds or crates. This is best ignored unless you catch him in the act—but always clean up thoroughly.

81

less, if you approach housebreaking your Beagle with total commitment and a positive attitude, you will have no more problem training this dog than you would any other breed.

Begin by selecting the relief surface that is most convenient for you and your living situation. You can train a puppy to relieve himself wherever you choose, but this must be somewhere suitable. Outdoor training includes such surfaces as grass, soil and cement. Indoor training usually means training your dog to newspaper. When deciding on the surface and location that you will want your Beagle to use, be sure it is going to be permanent. Training your dog to grass and then changing

Beagles are excellent scent-hounds and they usually search the area for interesting odors and "messages" from other dogs.

PAPER CAPER

Never line your pup's sleeping area with newspaper. Litters are usually raised on newspaper and, once in your home, the puppy will immediately associate newspaper with voiding. Never put newspaper on any floor while house-training, as this will only confuse the puppy. If you are paper-training him, use paper in his designated relief area only.

your mind two months later is extremely difficult for both dog and owner. You should bear in mind from the outset that when your puppy is old enough to go out in public places, any canine deposits must be removed at once. You will always have to carry with you a small plastic bag or "poop-scoop."

Many trainers advise using a verbal command to encourage the pup to relieve himself. Choose the command you will

CANINE DEVELOPMENT SCHEDULE

It is important to understand how and at what age a puppy develops into adulthood. If you are a puppy owner, consult the following Canine Development Schedule to determine the stage of development your puppy is currently experiencing. This knowledge will help you as you work with the puppy in the weeks and months ahead.

Period	Age	Characteristics
FIRST TO THIRD	BIRTH TO SEVEN WEEKS	Puppy needs food, sleep and warmth, and responds to simple and gentle touching. Needs mother for security and disciplining. Needs littermates for learning and interacting with other dogs. Pup learns to function within a pack and learns pack order of dominance. Begin socializing with adults and children for short periods. Begins to become aware of his environment.
FOURTH	EIGHT TO TWELVE WEEKS	Brain is fully developed. Needs socializing with outside world. Remove from mother and littermates. Needs to change from canine pack to human pack. Human dominance necessary. Fear period occurs between 8 and 16 weeks. Avoid fright and pain.
FIFTH	THIRTEEN TO SIXTEEN WEEKS	Training and formal obedience should begin. Less association with other dogs, more with people, places, situations. Period will pass easily if you remember this is pup's change-to-adolescence time. Be firm and fair. Flight instinct prominent. Permissiveness and over-disciplining can do permanent damage. Praise for good behavior.
JUVENILE	FOUR TO EIGHT MONTHS	Another fear period about 7 to 8 months of age. It passes quickly, but be cautious of fright and pain. Sexual maturity reached. Dominant traits established. Dog should understand sit, down, come and stay by now.

NOTE: THESE ARE APPROXIMATE TIME FRAMES. ALLOW FOR INDIVIDUAL DIFFERENCES IN PUPPIES.

use each and every time you want your puppy to void. "Hurry up" and "Let's go" are examples of commands commonly used by dog owners. Get in the habit of giving the puppy your chosen relief command before you take him out. That way, when he becomes an adult, you will be able to determine if he wants to go out when you ask him. A confirmation will be signs of interest such as wagging his tail, watching you intently, going to the door, etc.

PUPPY'S NEEDS

The puppy needs to relieve himself after play periods, after each meal, after he has been sleeping and at any time he indicates that he is looking for a place to urinate or defecate.

The urinary and intestinal tract muscles of very young puppies are not fully developed. Therefore, like human babies, puppies need to relieve

Always use a poop-scoop to clean up your dog's mess.

HOW MANY TIMES A DAY?

AGE	RELIEF TRIPS
To 14 weeks	10
14–22 weeks	8
22–32 weeks	6
Adulthood (dog stops growing)	4

These are estimates, of course, but they are a guide to the minimum number of opportunities a dog should have each day to relieve himself.

themselves frequently. Take your puppy out often—every hour for an eight-week-old Beagle, for example, and always immediately after sleeping and eating. The older the puppy, the less often he will need to relieve himself. Finally, as a mature healthy adult, he will require only three to five relief trips per day.

HOUSING

Since the types of housing and control you provide for your puppy have a direct relationship on the success of house-training, we consider the various aspects of both before we begin training.

Bringing a new puppy home and turning him loose in your house can be compared to turning a child loose in a sports arena and telling the child that the place is all his! The sheer enormity of the place would be too much for him to handle.

Instead, offer the puppy clearly defined areas where he can play, sleep, eat and live. A room of the house where the family gathers is the most obvious choice. Puppies are social animals and need to feel a part of the pack right from the start. Hearing your voice, watching you while you are doing things and smelling you nearby are all positive reinforcers that he is now a member of your pack. Usually a family room, the kitchen or a nearby adjoining breakfast area is ideal for providing safety and security for both puppy and owner.

Within that room, there should be a smaller area that the puppy can call his own. An alcove, a wire or fiberglass dog crate or a fenced (not boarded!) corner from which he can view the activities of his new family will be fine. The size of the area

Keeping your own yard clean is just as important as picking up after your dog in public.

or crate is the key factor here. The area must be large enough for the puppy to lie down and stretch out as well as stand up without rubbing his head on the top, yet small enough so that he cannot relieve himself at one end and sleep at the other without coming into contact with his droppings before he is fully trained to relieve himself outside.

Dogs are, by nature, clean animals and will not remain close to their relief areas unless forced to do so. In those cases, they then become dirty dogs and usually remain that way for life.

The designated area should be lined with clean bedding and a toy. Water must always be available, in a non-spill container,

Practice is the answer. This Beagle is practicing with a collapsed tunnel, one of the obstacles in an agility trial.

THE GOLDEN RULE

The golden rule of dog training is simple. For each "question" (command), there is only one correct answer (reaction). One command = one reaction. Keep practicing the command until the dog reacts correctly without hesitating. Be repetitive but not monotonous. Dogs get bored just as people do!

but you should monitor your Beagle's water intake during house-training so you'll know when he'll need "to go."

CONTROL

By control, we mean helping the puppy to create a lifestyle pattern that will be compatible to that of his human pack (*you!*). Just as we guide little children to learn our way of life, we must show the puppy when it is time to play, eat, sleep, exercise and even entertain himself.

Your puppy should always sleep in his crate. He should also learn that, during times of household confusion and excessive human activity such as at breakfast when family members are preparing for the day, he can play by himself in relative safety and comfort in his designated area. Each time you leave the puppy alone, he should understand exactly where he is to stay. You can gradually increase the time he is left alone to get him used to it.

This Beagle became accustomed to his crate as a young puppy. Now that he is a senior citizen, the crate offers him a protective haven in which to take a break from the bustle of everyday life.

Puppies are chewers. They cannot tell the difference between lamp cords, television wires, shoes, table legs, etc. Chewing into a television wire, for example, can be fatal to the pup, while a shorted wire can start a fire in the house.

If the puppy chews on the arm of the chair when he is alone, you will probably discipline him angrily when you get home. Thus, he makes the association that your coming home means he is going to be punished. (He will not remember chewing up the chair and is incapable of making the association of the discipline with his naughty deed.) Crating the pup prevents these situation from occurring.

Other times of excitement, such as family parties, friends' visits, etc., can be fun for the puppy, providing he can view the activities from the security of his designated area. He is not underfoot and he is not being fed all sorts of tidbits that will probably cause him stomach distress, yet he still feels a part of the fun.

SCHEDULE
A puppy should be taken to his relief area each time he is released from his designated area, after meals, after play sessions and when he first awakens in the morning (at age

HOUSEBREAKING TIP

Most of all, be consistent. Always take your dog to the same location, always use the same command and always have the dog on leash when he is in his relief area, unless a fenced-in yard is available.

By following the Success Method, your puppy will be completely housebroken by the time his muscle and brain development reach maturity. Keep in mind that small breeds usually mature faster than large breeds, but all puppies should be trained by six months of age.

eight weeks, this can mean 5 a.m.!). The puppy will indicate that he's ready "to go" by circling or sniffing busily—do not misinterpret these signs. For a puppy less than ten weeks of age, a routine of taking him out every hour is necessary. As the puppy grows, he will be able to wait for longer periods of time.

Keep trips to his relief area short. Stay no more than five or six minutes and then return to the house. If he goes during that time, praise him lavishly and take him indoors immediately. If he does not, but he has an accident when you go back indoors, pick him up immediately, say "No! No!" and return to his relief area. Wait a few minutes, then return to the

A helpful aid is a small pet door by which your Beagle can come and go as his needs indicate. One of the negatives of this sort of pet door is that it allows an unsecured opening into the house.

THE CLEAN LIFE

House-training is an endeavor of utmost importance with any breed of dog. By providing sleeping and resting quarters that fit the dog, and offering frequent opportunities to relieve himself outside his quarters, the puppy quickly learns that the outdoors (or the newspaper if you are training him to paper) is the place to go when he needs to urinate or defecate. It also reinforces his innate desire to keep his sleeping quarters clean. This, in turn, helps develop the muscle control that will eventually produce a dog with clean living habits. With a Beagle, it is essential to begin a house-training routine as soon as you bring the puppy home.

house again. Never hit a puppy or put his face in urine or excrement when he has an accident!

Once indoors, put the puppy in his crate until you have had time to clean up his accident. Then release him to the family area and watch him more closely than before. Chances are, his accident was a result of your not picking up his signal or waiting too long before offering him the opportunity to relieve himself. Never hold a grudge against the puppy for accidents.

Let the puppy learn that going outdoors means that it is time to relieve himself, not play. Once trained, he will be able to play indoors and out and still differentiate between the times for play versus the times for relief.

Help him develop regular hours for naps, being alone, playing by himself and just resting, all in his crate. Encourage him to entertain himself while you are busy with your activities. Let him learn that having you near is comforting, but it is not your main purpose in life to provide him with your undivided attention.

Each time you put a puppy in his crate, use the same command, whatever suits best. Soon, he will run to his crate or area when he hears you say those words.

Crate training provides safety for you, the puppy and the home. It also provides the puppy with a feeling of security, and that helps the puppy achieve self-confidence and clean habits.

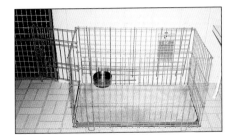

A wire crate offers your Beagle many advantages. It is ideal for use in the home, as most Beagles like to be able to see what's going on around them.

THE SUCCESS METHOD

Success that comes by luck is usually short-lived. Success that comes by well-thought-out proven methods is often more easily achieved and permanent. This is the Success Method. It is designed to give you, the puppy owner, a simple yet proven way to help your puppy develop clean living habits and a feeling of security in his new environment.

6 Steps to Successful Crate Training

1 Tell the puppy "Crate time!" and place him in the crate with a small treat (a piece of cheese or half of a biscuit). Let him stay in the crate for five minutes while you are in the same room. Then release him and praise lavishly. Never release him when he is fussing. Wait until he is quiet before you let him out.

2 Repeat Step 1 several times a day.

3 The next day, place the puppy in the crate as before. Let him stay there for ten minutes. Do this several times.

4 Continue building time in five-minute increments until the puppy stays in his crate for 30 minutes with you in the room. Always take him to his relief area after prolonged periods in his crate.

5 Now go back to Step 1 and let the puppy stay in his crate for five minutes, this time while you are out of the room.

6 Once again, build crate time in five-minute increments with you out of the room. When the puppy will stay willingly in his crate (he may even fall asleep!) for 30 minutes with you out of the room, he will be ready to stay in it for several hours at a time.

Remember that one of the primary ingredients in house-training your puppy is control. Regardless of your lifestyle, there will always be occasions when you will need to have a place where your dog can stay and be happy and safe. Crate training is the answer for now and in the future.

In conclusion, a few key elements are really all you need for a successful house-training method—consistency, frequency, praise, control and supervision. By following these procedures with a normal, healthy puppy, you and the puppy will soon be past the stage of "accidents" and ready to move on to a full and rewarding life together.

ROLES OF DISCIPLINE, REWARD AND PUNISHMENT

Discipline, training one to act in accordance with rules, brings

Crate training is the singular most important training you give your Beagle. You will reap the rewards and convenience of crate training during your dog's entire life.

order to life. It is as simple as that. Without discipline, particularly in a group society, chaos reigns supreme and the group will eventually perish. Humans and canines are social animals and need some form of discipline in order to function effectively. They must procure food, protect their home base and their young and reproduce to keep the species going.

If there were no discipline in the lives of social animals, they would eventually die from starvation and/or predation by other, stronger animals.

In the case of domestic canines, dogs need discipline in their lives in order to understand how their pack (you and other family members) functions and how they must act in order to survive.

A large humane society in a

highly populated area recently surveyed dog owners regarding their satisfaction with their relationships with their dogs. People who had trained their dogs were 75% more satisfied with their pets than those who had never trained their dogs.

Dr. Edward Thorndike, a psychologist, established *Thorndike's Theory of Learning*, which states that a behavior that results in a pleasant event tends to be repeated. A behavior that results in an unpleasant event tends not to be repeated. It is this theory on which training methods are based today. For example, if you manipulate a dog to perform a specific behavior and reward him for doing it, he is likely to do it again because he enjoyed the end result.

Occasionally, punishment, a penalty inflicted for an offense, is necessary. The best type of punishment often comes from an outside source. For example, a child is told not to touch the stove because he may get burned. He disobeys and touches the stove. In doing so, he receives a burn. From that time on, he respects the heat of the stove and avoids contact with it. Therefore, a behavior that results in an unpleasant event tends not to be repeated.

A good example of a dog's learning the hard way is the dog

PRACTICE MAKES PERFECT

• Have training lessons with your dog every day in several short segments—three to five times a day for a few minutes at a time is ideal.

• Do not have long practice sessions. The dog will become easily bored.

• Never practice when you are tired, ill, worried or in an otherwise negative mood. This will transmit to the dog and may have an adverse effect on his performance.

Think fun, short and above all positive! End each session on a high note, rather than a failed exercise.

who chases the house cat. He is told many times to leave the cat alone, yet he persists in teasing the cat. Then, one day he begins chasing the cat but the cat turns and swipes a claw across the dog's face, leaving him with a painful gash on his nose. The

A lightweight yet sturdy leash and collar are ideal for everyday walks and training.

final result is that the dog stops chasing the cat.

TRAINING EQUIPMENT

COLLAR AND LEASH
For a Beagle, the collar and leash that you use for training must be one with which you are easily able to work, not too heavy for the dog and perfectly safe.

TREATS
Have a bag of treats on hand. Something nutritious and easy to swallow works best. Use a soft treat, a chunk of cheese or a piece of cooked chicken rather than a dry biscuit. By the time

the dog has finished chewing a dry treat, he will forget why he is being rewarded in the first place! Using food rewards will not teach a dog to beg at the table—the only way to teach a dog to beg at the table is to give him food from the table. In training, rewarding the dog with a food treat will help him associate praise and the treats with learning new behaviors that obviously please his owner.

TRAINING BEGINS: ASK THE DOG A QUESTION
In order to teach your dog anything, you must first get his attention. After all, he cannot learn anything if he is looking away from you with his mind on something else.

To get his attention, ask him "School?" and immediately walk over to him and give him a treat as you tell him "Good dog."

REAP THE REWARDS

If you start with a normal, healthy dog and give him time, patience and some carefully executed lessons, you will reap the rewards of that training for the life of the dog. And what a life it will be! The two of you will find immeasurable pleasure in the companionship you have built together with love, respect and mutual understanding.

KEEP SMILING

Never train your dog, puppy or adult, when you are angry or in a sour mood. Dogs are very sensitive to human feelings, especially anger, and if your dog senses that you are angry or upset, he will connect your anger with his training and learn to resent or fear his training sessions.

Wait a minute or two and repeat the routine, this time with a treat in your hand as you approach within a foot of the dog. Do not go directly to him, but stop about a foot short of him and hold out the treat as you ask "School?" He will see you approaching with a treat in your hand and most likely begin walking toward you. As you meet, give him the treat and praise again.

The third time, ask the question, have a treat in your hand and walk only a short distance toward the dog so that he must walk almost all the way to you. As he reaches you, give him the treat and praise again.

By this time, the dog will probably be getting the idea that if he pays attention to you, especially when you ask that question, it will pay off in treats and fun activities for him. In other words, he learns that "school" means doing fun things

with you that result in treats and positive attention for him.

Remember that the dog does not understand your verbal language; he only recognizes sounds. Your question translates to a series of sounds for him, and those sounds become the signal to go to you and pay attention; if he does, he will get to interact with you plus receive treats and praise.

THE BASIC COMMANDS

TEACHING SIT

Now that you have the dog's attention, attach his leash and hold it in your left hand and a food treat in your right. Place your food hand at the dog's nose and let him lick the treat but not take it from you. Say "Sit" and slowly raise your food hand from in front of the dog's nose

Reward training is automatic. Give your Beagle a tasty treat and he'll do almost anything to please you. Beagles are almost always hungry, making training that much easier!

93

up over his head so that he is looking at the ceiling. As he bends his head upward, he will have to bend his knees to maintain his balance. As he bends his knees, he will assume a sit position. At that point, release the food treat and praise lavishly with comments such as "Good dog! Good sit!," etc. Remember to always praise enthusiastically, because dogs relish verbal praise from their owners and feel so proud of themselves whenever they accomplish a behavior.

A potential show dog should be trained to "stack" or "stand," using a treat to hold his attention. Many handlers use treats in the show ring for the same purpose.

You will not use food forever in getting the dog to obey your commands. Food is only used to teach new behaviors, and once the dog knows what you want when you give a specific command, you will wean him off the food treats but still maintain the verbal praise. After all, you will always have your

THE COCOA WARS

Chocolate contains the chemical thebromine, which is poisonous to dogs, although "chocolates" especially made for dogs are safe (as they don't actually contain chocolate) but not recommended. Any item that encourages your dog to enjoy the taste of cocoa should be discouraged. You should also exercise caution when using mulch in your garden. This frequently contains cocoa hulls, and dogs have been known to die from eating the mulch.

voice with you, and there will be many times when you have no food rewards but expect the dog to obey.

TEACHING DOWN

Teaching the down exercise is easy when you understand how the dog perceives the down position, and it is very difficult when you do not. Dogs perceive the down position as a submissive one; therefore, teaching the down exercise using a forceful method can sometimes make the dog develop such a fear of the down that he either runs away when you say "Down" or he attempts to snap at the person who tries to force him down.

Have the dog sit close alongside your left leg, facing in the same direction as you are.

begin moving it forward along the floor in front of the dog. Keep talking softly to the dog, saying things like, "Do you want this treat? You can do this, good dog." Your reassuring tone of voice will help calm the dog as he tries to follow the food hand in order to get the treat.

When the dog's elbows touch the floor, release the food and praise softly. Try to get the dog to maintain that down position for several seconds before you

Sit is a natural position for your dog and can be taught effectively with a handful of treats and heartful of patience.

Whenever your Beagle obeys a command, praise him lavishly to encourage a repeat performance.

Hold the leash in your left hand and a food treat in your right. Now place your left hand lightly on the top of the dog's shoulders where they meet above the spinal cord. Do not push down on the dog's shoulders; simply rest your left hand there so you can guide the dog to lie down close to your left leg rather than to swing away from your side when he drops.

Now place the food hand at the dog's nose, say "Down" very softly (almost a whisper) and slowly lower the food hand to the dog's front feet. When the food hand reaches the floor,

95

treat in your right hand and place your food hand at the dog's nose. Say "Stay" and step out on your right foot to stand directly in front of the dog, toe to toe, as he licks and nibbles the treat. Be sure to keep his head facing upward to maintain the sit position. Count to five and then swing around to stand next to the dog again with him on your left. As soon as you get back to the original position, release the food and praise lavishly.

As the dog looks up to follow your hand, he naturally assumes the sit position.

let him sit up again. The goal here is to get the dog to settle down and not feel threatened in the down position.

TEACHING STAY

It is easy to teach the dog to stay in either a sit or a down position. Again, we use food and praise during the teaching process as we help the dog to understand exactly what it is that we are expecting him to do.

To teach the sit/stay, start with the dog sitting on your left side as before and hold the leash in your left hand. Have a food

DOUBLE JEOPARDY

A dog in jeopardy never lies down. He stays alert on his feet because instinct tells him that he may have to run away or fight for his survival. Therefore, if a dog feels threatened or anxious, he will not lie down. Consequently, it is important to keep the dog calm and relaxed as he learns the down exercise.

Use a combination of voice and hand signals to teach your Beagle to stay.

in your right hand as before, but this time the food is not touching the dog's nose. He will watch the food hand and quickly learn that he is going to get that treat as soon as you return to his side.

When you can stand 3 feet away from your dog for 30 seconds, you can then begin building time and distance in both stays. Eventually, the dog can be expected to remain in the stay position for prolonged periods of time until you return to him or call him to you. Always praise lavishly when he stays.

TEACHING COME

If you make teaching "come" a fun experience, you should never have a "student" that does not love the game or that fails to come when called. The secret, it seems, is never to teach the word "come."

To teach the down/stay, do the down as previously described. As soon as the dog lies down, say "Stay" and step out on your right foot just as you did in the sit/stay. Count to five and then return to stand beside the dog with him on your left side. Release the treat and praise as always.

Within a week or ten days, you can begin to add a bit of distance between you and your dog when you leave him. When you do, use your left hand open with the palm facing the dog as a stay signal, much the same as the hand signal a police officer uses to stop traffic at an intersection. Hold the food treat

PLAY FETCH

Play fetching games with your puppy in an enclosed area where he can fetch his toy and bring it back to you. Always use a toy or object designated just for this purpose. Never use a shoe, sock or other item he may later confuse with those in your closet or underneath your chair.

97

At times when an owner most wants his dog to come when called, the owner is likely upset or anxious and he allows these feelings to come through in the tone of his voice when he calls his dog. Hearing that desperation in his owner's voice, the dog fears the results of going to him and therefore either disobeys outright or runs in the opposite direction. The secret, therefore, is to teach the dog a game and, when you want him to come to you, simply play the game. It is practically a no-fail solution!

To begin, have several members of your family take a few food treats and each go into a different room in the house. Take turns calling the dog, and each person should celebrate the dog's finding him with a treat

"COME" . . . BACK

Never call your dog to come to you for a correction or scold him when he reaches you. That is the quickest way to turn a come command into "Go away fast!" Dogs think only in the present tense, and your dog will connect the scolding with coming to you, not with the misbehavior of a few moments earlier.

"WHERE ARE YOU?"

When calling the dog, do not say "Come." Say things like, "Rover, where are you? See if you can find me! I have a biscuit for you!" Keep up a constant line of chatter with coaxing sounds and frequent questions such as, "Where are you?" The dog will learn to follow the sound of your voice to locate you, and he will come running to receive his reward.

and lots of happy praise. When a person calls the dog, he is actually inviting the dog to find him and get a treat as a reward for "winning."

A few turns of the "Where are you?" game and the dog will understand that everyone is playing the game and that each person has a big celebration awaiting the dog's success at locating him. Once the dog learns to love the game, simply calling out "Where are you?" will bring him running from wherever he is when he hears

that all-important question.

The come command is recognized as one of the most important things to teach a dog, but there are trainers who work with thousands of dogs and never teach the actual word "come." Yet these dogs will race to respond to a person who uses the dog's name followed by "Where are you?" For example, a woman has a 12-year-old companion dog who went blind, but who never fails to locate her owner when asked, "Where are you?"

Children particularly love to play this game with their dogs. Children can hide in smaller places like a shower or bathtub, behind a bed or under a table. The dog needs to work a little bit harder to find these hiding places, but, when he does, he

Your Beagle will respond with excitement when he knows you are looking for him. The game-type approach to teaching the dog to "come" usually proves very successful.

Encouraging your Beagle to fetch a toy and bring it to you can be used to reinforce the behavior of coming when called.

99

loves to celebrate with a treat and a tussle with a favorite youngster.

TEACHING HEEL

Heeling means that the dog walks beside the owner without pulling. It takes time and patience on the owner's part to succeed at teaching the dog that he (the owner) will not proceed unless the dog is walking calmly beside him. Pulling out ahead on the leash is definitely not acceptable.

Begin with holding the leash in your left hand as the dog sits beside your left leg. Move the loop end of the leash to your right hand but keep your left hand short on the leash so it keeps the dog in close next to you.

Say "Heel" and step forward on your left foot. Keep the dog close to you and take three steps. Stop and have the dog sit next to you in what we now call

the heel position. Praise verbally, but do not touch the dog. Hesitate a moment and begin again with "Heel," taking three steps and stopping, at which point the dog is told to sit again.

Your goal here is to have the dog walk those three steps without pulling on the leash. Once he will walk calmly beside you for three steps without pulling, increase the number of steps you take to five. When he will walk politely beside you while you take five steps, you can increase the length of your walk to ten steps. Keep increasing the length of your stroll until the dog will walk quietly beside you without pulling as long as you want him to heel. When you stop heeling, indicate to the dog that the exercise is over by verbally praising as you pet him and say, "OK, good dog." The "OK" is used as a release word, meaning that the exercise is finished and the dog is free to relax.

If you are dealing with a dog who insists on pulling you around, simply "put on your brakes" and stand your ground until the dog realizes that the two of you are not going anywhere until he is beside you and moving at your pace, not his. It may take some time just standing there to convince the dog that you are the leader and

TUG OF WALK?

If you begin teaching the heel by taking long walks and letting the dog pull you along, he misinterprets this action as an acceptable form of taking a walk. When you pull back on the lead to counteract his pulling, he reads that tug as a signal to pull even harder!

HEELING WELL

Teach your dog to heel in an enclosed area. Once you think the dog will obey reliably and you want to attempt advanced obedience exercises such as off-lead heeling, test him in a fenced-in area so he cannot run away.

you will be the one to decide on the direction and speed of your travel.

Each time the dog looks up at you or slows down to give a slack leash between the two of you, quietly praise him and say, "Good heel. Good dog." Eventually, the dog will begin to respond and within a few days he will be walking politely beside you without pulling on the leash. At first, the training sessions should be kept short and very positive; soon, the dog will be able to walk nicely with you for increasingly longer distances. Remember also to give the dog free time and the opportunity to run and play when you have finished heel practice.

WEANING OFF FOOD IN TRAINING

Food is used in training new behaviors. Once the dog understands what behavior goes with a specific command, it is time to start weaning him off the food treats. At first, give a treat after each exercise. Then, start to give a treat only after every other exercise. Mix up the times when you offer a food reward and the times when you only offer praise so that the dog will never know when he is going to receive both food and praise and when he is going to receive only praise. This is called a variable ratio reward system and it proves successful because there is always the chance that the owner will produce a treat, so the dog never stops trying for that reward. No matter what, *always* give verbal praise.

OBEDIENCE CLASSES

It is a good idea to enroll in an obedience class if one is available in your area. If yours is a show dog, handling classes would be also appropriate to prepare both of you for the ring. Many areas have dog clubs that offer basic obedience training as well as preparatory classes for obedience competition. Local dog trainers also offer similar classes.

At obedience trials, dogs can earn titles at various levels of competition. The beginning levels of competition include basic behaviors such as sit, down, heel, etc. The more advanced levels of competition include jumping, retrieving,

101

You won't use treats in training forever, but it makes it easier to get a pup's attention when starting out.

scent discrimination and signal work. The advanced levels require a dog and owner to put a lot of time and effort into their training, and the titles that can be earned at these levels of competition are very prestigious.

A BORN PRODIGY

If your intent is to show your Beagle, start training him in the proper pose as soon as you have taught him the basic commands.

Occasionally, a dog and owner who have not attended formal classes have been able to earn entry-level titles by obtaining competition rules and regulations from a local kennel club and practicing on their own to a degree of perfection. Obtaining the higher level titles, however, almost always requires extensive training under the tutelage of experienced instructors. In addition, the more difficult levels require more special-ized equipment whereas the lower levels do not.

OTHER ACTIVITIES FOR LIFE
Whether a dog is trained in the structured environment of a class or alone with his owner at home, there are many activities that can bring fun and rewards to both owner and dog once they have mastered basic control.

Teaching the dog to help out around the home, in the yard or on the farm provides great satisfaction to both dog and owner. In addition, the dog's help makes life a little easier for his owner and raises his stature as a valued companion to his

family. It helps give the dog a purpose by occupying his mind and providing an outlet for his energy.

If you are interested in participating in organized competition with your Beagle, there are activities other than obedience in which you and your dog can become involved. Agility, for example, is a popular and fun sport in which dogs run through an obstacle course that includes various jumps, tunnels and other exercises to test the dog's speed and coordination. The owners run through the course beside their dogs to give commands and to guide them through the course. Although competitive, the focus is on fun—it's fun to do, fun to watch and great exercise.

There are many activities in which you and your Beagle can participate. Contact your local dog club to learn more details about trials, tests and other organized canine competitions.

The Beagle's natural energy and instinctive skills enable him to be trained for and fare well in many types of dog sports and activities.

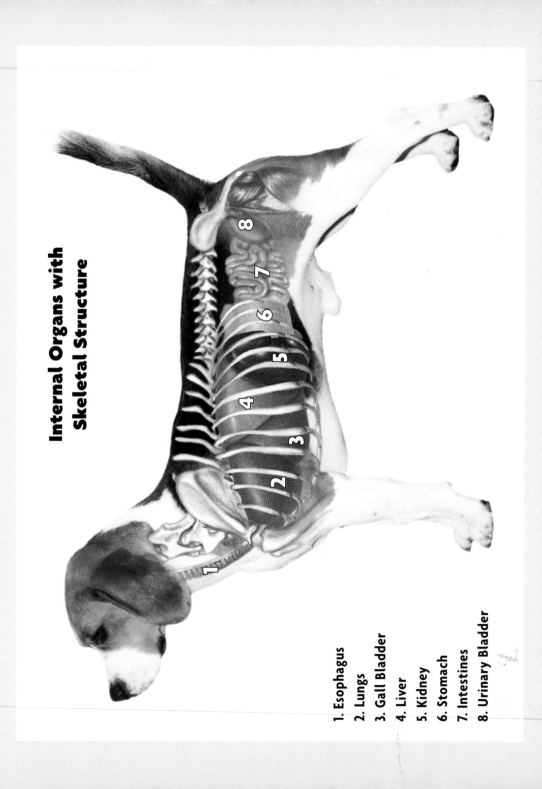

Internal Organs with Skeletal Structure

1. Esophagus
2. Lungs
3. Gall Bladder
4. Liver
5. Kidney
6. Stomach
7. Intestines
8. Urinary Bladder

HEALTH CARE OF YOUR
BEAGLE

Dogs suffer from many of the same physical illnesses as people. They might even share many of the same psychological problems. Since people usually know more about human diseases than canine maladies, many of the terms used in this chapter will be familiar but not necessarily those used by veterinarians. We will use the term *x-ray*, instead of the more acceptable term *radiograph*. We will also use the familiar term *symptoms* even though dogs don't have symptoms, which are verbal descriptions of the patient's feelings; dogs have *clinical signs*. Since dogs can't speak, we have to look for clinical signs...but we still use the term *symptoms* in this book.

As a general rule, medicine is *practiced*. That term is not arbitrary. Medicine is a constantly changing art as we learn more and more about genetics, electronic aids (like CAT scans and MRIs) and daily laboratory advances. There are many dog maladies, like hip dysplasia, which are not universally treated in the same manner.

SELECTING A QUALIFIED VET
Your selection of a veterinarian should be based not only upon personality and skills but also upon his convenience to your home. You want a vet who is close because you might have emergencies or need to make multiple visits for treatments. You want a vet who has sophisticated pet supplies and a good reputation for ability and responsiveness. There is nothing more frustrating than having to wait a day or more to get a response from your veterinarian.

A qualified veterinarian is able to provide your Beagle with all the care he requires, including recommendations for specialized testing and treatment if necessary.

All veterinarians are licensed and their diplomas and/or certificates should be displayed in their waiting

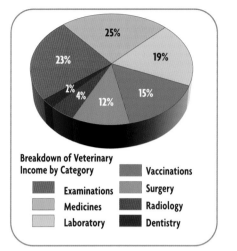

A typical vet's income, categorized according to services performed. This survey dealt with small-animal (pet) practices.

25%

19%

23%

2% 4%

15%

12%

Breakdown of Veterinary Income by Category

- Vaccinations
- Examinations
- Surgery
- Medicines
- Radiology
- Laboratory
- Dentistry

rooms. There are, however, many veterinary specialties that usually require further studies and internships. There are specialists in heart problems (veterinary cardiologists), skin problems (veterinary dermatologists), teeth and gum problems (veterinary dentists), eye problems (veterinary ophthalmologists) and x-rays (veterinary radiologists), as well as surgeons who have specialties in bones, muscles or certain organs. Most veterinarians do routine surgery such as

neutering, stitching up wounds and docking tails for those breeds in which such is required for show purposes. When the problem affecting your dog is serious, it is not unusual or impudent to get another medical opinion, although it is courteous to advise the vets concerned about this. You might also want to compare costs among several veterinarians. Sophisticated health care and veterinary services can be very costly. Don't be bashful about discussing these costs with your veterinarian or his staff. It is not infrequent that important decisions are based upon financial considerations.

PREVENTATIVE MEDICINE
It is much easier, less costly and more effective to practice preventative medicine than to fight bouts of illness and disease. Properly bred puppies come from parents that were selected based upon their genetic-disease profiles. Their mother should have been vaccinated, free of all internal and external parasites and properly nourished. For these reasons, a visit to the veterinarian who cared for the dam is recommended. The dam can pass on disease resistance to her puppies, which can last for eight to ten weeks. She can also pass on parasites and many infections. That's why it is helpful to learn as much about the dam's health as possible.

CUSHING'S DISEASE

Cases of hyperactive adrenal glands (Cushing's disease) have been traced to the drinking of highly chlorinated water. Aerate or age your dog's drinking water before offering it.

First Aid at a Glance

Burns
Place the affected area under cool water; use ice if only a small area is burnt.

Bee stings/Insect bites
Apply ice to relieve swelling; antihistamine dosed properly.

Animal bites
Clean any bleeding area; apply pressure until bleeding subsides; go to the vet.

Spider bites
Use cold compress and a pressurized pack to inhibit venom's spreading.

Antifreeze poisoning
Immediately induce vomiting by using hydrogen peroxide.

Fish hooks
Removal best handled by vet; hook must be cut in order to remove.

Snake bites
Pack ice around bite; contact vet quickly; identify snake for proper antivenin.

Car accident
Move dog from roadway with blanket; seek veterinary aid.

Shock
Calm the dog, keep him warm; seek immediate veterinary help.

Nosebleed
Apply cold compress to the nose; apply pressure to any visible abrasion.

Bleeding
Apply pressure above the area; treat wound by applying a cotton pack.

Heat stroke
Submerge dog in cold bath; cool down with fresh air and water; go to the vet.

Frostbite/Hypothermia
Warm the dog with a warm bath, electric blankets or hot water bottles.

Abrasions
Clean the wound and wash out thoroughly with fresh water; apply antiseptic.

!! *Remember: an injured dog may attempt to bite a helping hand from fear and confusion. Always muzzle the dog before trying to offer assistance.* !!

WEANING TO FIVE MONTHS OLD

Puppies should be weaned by the time they are about two months old. A puppy that remains for at least eight weeks with his mother and littermates usually adapts better to other dogs and people later in his life.

Some new owners have their puppies examined by a veterinarian immediately, which is a good idea unless a puppy is overtired by the ride home. Vaccination programs usually begin when the puppy is very young.

The puppy will have his teeth examined and have his skeletal conformation and general health checked prior to certification by the veterinarian. Puppies in certain breeds have problems with their kneecaps, cataracts and other eye problems, heart murmurs and undescended testicles. They may also have personality problems,

MORE THAN VACCINES

Vaccinations help prevent your new puppy from contracting diseases, but they do not cure them. Proper nutrition as well as parasite control keep your dog healthy and less susceptible to many dangerous diseases. Remember that your dog depends on you and your veterinarian to ensure his health and continued well-being.

and your veterinarian might have training in temperament testing.

VACCINATION SCHEDULING

Most vaccinations are given by injection and should only be done by a veterinarian. Both he and you should keep a record of the date of the injection, the identification of the vaccine and the amount given. Some vets give a first vaccination at eight weeks, but most dog breeders prefer the course not to commence until about ten weeks because of the risk of negating any antibodies passed on by the dam. The vaccination scheduling is usually based on a 15-day cycle. You must take your vet's advice as to when to vaccinate, as this may differ according to the vaccine used.

Most vaccinations immunize your puppy against viruses. The usual vaccines contain immunizing doses of several different viruses such as distemper, parvovirus, parainfluenza and hepatitis. There are other vaccines available when the puppy is at risk. You should rely upon professional advice. This is especially true for the booster-shot program. Most vaccination programs require a booster when the puppy is a year old and once a year thereafter. In some cases, circumstances may require more or less frequent immunizations.

Canine cough, more formally known as tracheobronchitis, is treated with a vaccine that is sprayed into the dog's nostrils.

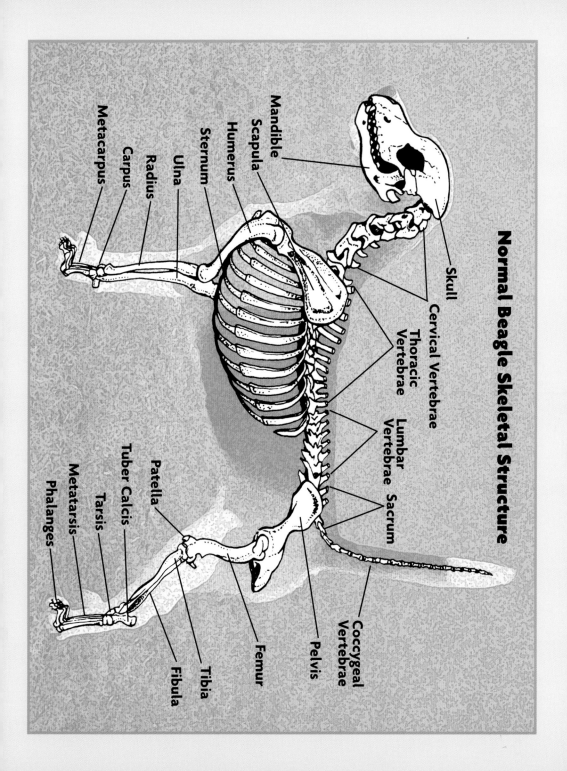

Normal Beagle Skeletal Structure

Metacarpus
Carpus
Radius
Ulna
Sternum
Humerus
Scapula
Mandible

Skull
Cervical Vertebrae
Thoracic Vertebrae
Lumbar Vertebrae
Sacrum
Coccygeal Vertebrae
Pelvis

Phalanges
Metatarsis
Tarsis
Tuber Calcis
Patella
Fibula
Tibia
Femur

HEALTH AND VACCINATION SCHEDULE

AGE IN WEEKS:	3RD	6TH	8TH	10TH	12TH	14TH	16TH	20-24TH
Worm Control	✔	✔	✔	✔	✔	✔	✔	✔
Neutering								✔
Heartworm		✔						✔
Parvovirus		✔		✔		✔		✔
Distemper			✔		✔		✔	
Hepatitis			✔		✔		✔	
Leptospirosis		✔		✔		✔		
Parainfluenza		✔		✔		✔		
Dental Examination			✔					✔
Complete Physical			✔					✔
Temperament Testing			✔					
Coronavirus					✔			
Canine Cough		✔						
Hip Dysplasia							✔	
Rabies								✔

Vaccinations are not instantly effective. It takes about two weeks for the dog's immune system to develop antibodies. Most vaccinations require annual booster shots. Your veterinarian should guide you in this regard.

Canine cough is usually included in routine vaccination, but this is often not as effective as those for other major diseases.

FIVE MONTHS TO ONE YEAR OF AGE
Unless you intend to breed or show your dog, neutering the puppy at six months of age is recommended. Discuss this with your veterinarian; most professionals advise neutering the male puppy and spaying the female puppy. Neutering has proven to be extremely beneficial to both males and females. Besides eliminating the possibility of pregnancy, it inhibits (but does not prevent) breast cancer in bitches and prostate cancer in male dogs. It is very rare to diagnose breast cancer in a female dog who was spayed at or before about nine months of age before her first heat.

OVER ONE YEAR OF AGE
Once a year, your grown dog should visit the vet for an examination and vaccination boosters. Some vets recommend blood tests, thyroid level check and dental evaluation to accompany these annual visits. A thorough clinical evaluation by the vet can provide critical background information for your dog. Blood tests are often performed at one year of age, and

dental examinations around the third or fourth birthday. In the long run, quality preventive care for your pet can save money, teeth and lives.

SKIN PROBLEMS IN BEAGLES

Veterinarians are consulted by dog owners for skin problems more than for any other group of diseases or maladies. Dogs' skin is almost as sensitive as human skin and both suffer from almost the same ailments (though the occurrence of acne in most breeds of dog

VACCINE ALLERGIES

It is important to begin a vaccination program with your puppy. However, Vaccines do not work all the time. Sometimes dogs are allergic to them and many times the antibodies, which are supposed to be stimulated by the vaccine, just are not produced. You should keep your dog in the veterinary clinic for an hour after it is vaccinated to be sure there are no allergic reactions.

DISEASE REFERENCE CHART

	What is it?	What causes it?	Symptoms
Leptospirosis	Severe disease that affects the internal organs; can be spread to people.	A bacterium, which is often carried by rodents, that enters through mucous membranes and spreads quickly throughout the body.	Range from fever, vomiting and loss of appetite in less severe cases to shock, irreversible kidney damage and possibly death in most severe cases.
Rabies	Potentially deadly virus that infects warm-blooded mammals.	Bite from a carrier of the virus, mainly wild animals.	1st stage: dog exhibits change in behavior, fear. 2nd stage: dog's behavior becomes more aggressive. 3rd stage: loss of coordination, trouble with bodily functions.
Parvovirus	Highly contagious virus, potentially deadly.	Ingestion of the virus, which is usually spread through the feces of infected dogs.	Most common: severe diarrhea. Also vomiting, fatigue, lack of appetite.
Canine cough	Contagious respiratory infection.	Combination of types of bacteria and virus. Most common: *Bordetella bronchiseptica* bacteria and parainfluenza virus.	Chronic cough.
Distemper	Disease primarily affecting respiratory and nervous system.	Virus that is related to the human measles virus.	Mild symptoms such as fever, lack of appetite and mucous secretion progress to evidence of brain damage, "hard pad."
Hepatitis	Virus primarily affecting the liver.	Canine adenovirus type I (CAV-1). Enters system when dog breathes in particles.	Lesser symptoms include listlessness, diarrhea, vomiting. More severe symptoms include "blue-eye" (clumps of virus in eye).
Coronavirus	Virus resulting in digestive problems.	Virus is spread through infected dog's feces.	Stomach upset evidenced by lack of appetite, vomiting, diarrhea.

is rare!). For this reason, veterinary dermatology has developed into a specialty practiced by many veterinarians.

Since many skin problems have visual symptoms that are almost identical, it requires the skill of an experienced veterinary dermatologist to identify and cure many of the more severe skin disorders. Pet shops sell many treatments for skin problems but most of the treatments are directed at symptoms and not the underlying problem(s). If your dog is suffering from a skin disorder, you should seek professional assistance as quickly as possible. As with all diseases, the earlier a problem is identified and treated, the more successful can be the cure.

PARASITE BITES
Many of us are allergic to insect bites. The bites itch, erupt and may even become infected. Dogs have the same reaction to fleas, ticks and/or mites. When an insect lands on you, you have the chance to whisk it away with your hand. Unfortunately, when your dog is bitten by a flea, tick or mite, it can only scratch it away or bite it. By the time the dog has been bitten, the parasite has done some of its damage. It may also have laid eggs, which will cause further problems in the near future. The itching from parasite bites is probably due to the saliva injected into the site when the parasite sucks the dog's blood.

AUTO-IMMUNE SKIN CONDITIONS
Auto-immune skin conditions are commonly referred to as being allergic to yourself, while allergies are usually inflammatory reactions to outside stimuli. Auto-immune diseases cause serious damage to the tissues that are involved.

The best known auto-immune disease is lupus, which affects people as well as dogs. The symptoms are variable and may affect the kidneys, bones, blood chemistry and skin. It can be fatal to both dogs and humans, though it is not thought to be transmissible. It is usually successfully treated

DENTAL HEALTH

A dental examination is in order when the dog is between six months and one year of age so that any permanent teeth that have erupted incorrectly can be corrected. It is important to begin a brushing routine, acclimate the puppy to brushing and be consistent for the duration of the dog's life. Durable nylon and safe edible chews should be a part of your puppy's arsenal for good health, good teeth and pleasant breath. The vast majority of dogs three to four years old and older has diseases of the gums from lack of dental attention. Using the various types of dental chews can be very effective in controlling dental plaque.

with cortisone, prednisone or a similar corticosteroid, but extensive use of these drugs can have harmful side effects.

AIRBORNE ALLERGIES

An interesting allergy is pollen allergy. Humans have hay fever, rose fever and other fevers from which they suffer during the pollinating season. Many dogs suffer from the same allergies. When the pollen count is high, your dog might suffer, but don't expect him to sneeze and have a runny nose like a human would. Dogs react to pollen allergies the same way they react to fleas—they scratch and bite themselves.

Dogs, like humans, can be tested for allergens. Discuss the testing with your veterinary dermatologist.

FOOD PROBLEMS

FOOD ALLERGIES

Dogs are allergic to many foods that are best-sellers and highly recommended by breeders and veterinarians. Changing the brand of food that you buy may not eliminate the problem if the element to which the dog is allergic is contained in the new brand.

Recognizing a food allergy is difficult. Humans vomit or have rashes when they eat a food to which they are allergic. Dogs neither vomit nor (usually) develop

Grass allergies and other airborne allergies are common ailments with Beagles as well as other breeds. Often the summer months are the worst for grass allergies, so wipe off your dog after he's been playing in the grass.

rashes. They react in the same manner as they do to an airborne or flea allergy: they itch, scratch and bite, thus making the diagnosis extremely difficult. While pollen allergies and parasite bites are usually seasonal, food allergies are year-round problems.

115

source of protein. Keep the dog on this diet (with no additives) for a month. If the symptoms of food allergy or intolerance disappear, chances are your dog has a food allergy.

Don't think that the single ingredient cured the problem. You still must find a suitable diet and ascertain which ingredient in the old diet was objectionable. This is most easily accomplished by adding ingredients to the new diet one at a time. Let the dog stay on the modified diet for a month before you add another ingredient. Eventually, you will determine the ingredient that caused the adverse reaction.

An alternative method is to carefully study the ingredients in the diet to which your dog is allergic or intolerant. Identify the main ingredient in this diet and eliminate the main ingredient by buying a different food that does not have that ingredient. Keep experimenting until the symptoms disappear after one month on the new diet.

Your Beagle can usually be maintained well on a complete commercial dog food. Any supplements to or changes in diet related to the dog's health, activity level, etc., should be discussed with the vet.

FOOD INTOLERANCE

Food intolerance is the inability of the dog to completely digest certain foods. For example, puppies that may have done very well on their mother's milk may not do well on cow's milk. The result of this food intolerance may be loose bowels, passing gas and stomach pains. These are the only obvious symptoms of food intolerance and that makes diagnosis difficult.

TREATING FOOD PROBLEMS

It is possible to handle food allergies and food intolerance yourself. Put your dog on a diet that he has never had. Obviously, if the dog has never eaten this new food, he can't have been allergic or intolerant of it. Start with a single ingredient that is not in the dog's diet at the present time. Ingredients like chopped beef or chicken are common in dog's diets, so try something more exotic like fish, rabbit or another

THE PROTEIN QUESTION

High activity level, stress, climate and other physical factors may require your dog to have more protein in his diet. Check with your veterinarian to ensure that the dog is receiving the correct balance, as too much protein can be harmful as well.

The great outdoors can mean encounters with insects and allergens, as well as the potential of ingesting something harmful. Always alert the vet if your Beagle starts to act or look ill.

A male dog flea,
*Ctenocephalides
canis.*

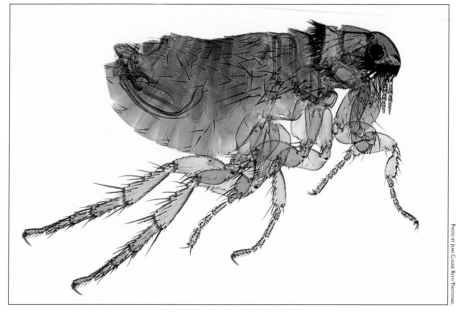

EXTERNAL PARASITES

FLEAS

Of all the problems to which dogs are prone, none is more well known and frustrating than fleas. Flea infestation is relatively simple to cure but difficult to prevent. Parasites that are harbored inside the body are a bit more difficult to eradicate but they are easier to control.

To control flea infestation, you have to understand the flea's life cycle. Fleas are often thought of as a summertime problem, but centrally heated homes have changed the patterns and fleas can be found at any time of the year. The most effective method of flea control is a two-stage approach: one stage to kill the adult fleas, and the other to control the development of pre-adult fleas. Unfortunately, no single active ingredient is effective against all stages of the life cycle.

FLEA KILLER CAUTION— "POISON"

Flea-killers are poisonous. You should not spray these toxic chemicals on areas of a dog's body that he licks, including his genitals and his face. Flea killers taken internally are a better answer, but check with your vet in case internal therapy is not advised for your dog.

LIFE CYCLE STAGES

During its life, a flea will pass through four life stages: egg, larva, pupa or nymph and adult. The adult stage is the most visible and irritating stage of the flea life cycle, and this is why the majority of flea-control products concentrate on this stage. The fact is that adult fleas account for only 1% of the total flea population, and the other 99% exist in pre-adult stages, i.e., eggs, larvae and nymphs. The pre-adult stages are barely visible to the naked eye.

THE LIFE CYCLE OF THE FLEA

Eggs are laid on the dog, usually in quantities of about 20 or 30, several times a day. The adult female flea must have a blood meal before each egg-laying session. When first laid, the eggs will cling to the dog's hair, as the eggs are still moist. However, they will quickly dry out and fall from the dog, especially if the dog moves around or scratches. Many eggs will fall off in the dog's favorite area or an area in which he spends a lot of time, such as his bed.

Once the eggs fall from the dog onto the carpet or furniture, they will hatch into larvae. This takes from one to ten days. Larvae are not particularly mobile and will usually travel only a few inches from where they hatch. However, they do have a tendency to move away from

EN GARDE: CATCHING FLEAS OFF GUARD!

Consider the following ways to arm yourself against fleas:
- Add a small amount of pennyroyal or eucalyptus oil to your dog's bath. These natural remedies repel fleas.
- Supplement your dog's food with fresh garlic (minced or grated) and a hearty amount of brewer's yeast, both of which ward off fleas.
- Use a flea comb on your dog daily. Submerge fleas in a cup of bleach to kill them quickly.
- Confine the dog to only a few rooms to limit the spread of fleas in the home.
- Vacuum daily...and get all of the crevices! Dispose of the bag every few days until the problem is under control.
- Wash your dog's bedding daily. Cover cushions where your dog sleeps with towels, and wash the towels often.

bright light and heavy traffic—under furniture and behind doors are common places to find high quantities of flea larvae.

The flea larvae feed on dead organic matter, including adult flea feces, until they are ready to change into adult fleas. Fleas will usually remain as larvae for around seven days. After this

PHOTO BY DWIGHT R. KUHN

Fleas have been measured as being able to jump 300,000 times and can jump over 150 times their length in any direction, including straight up.

period, the larvae will pupate into protective pupae. While inside the pupae, the larvae will undergo metamorphosis and change into adult fleas. This can take as little time as a few days, but the adult fleas can remain inside the pupae waiting to hatch for up to two years. The pupae are signaled to hatch by certain stimuli, such as physical pressure—the pupae's being stepped on, heat from an animal's lying on the pupae or increased carbon-dioxide levels and vibrations—indicating that a suitable host is available.

Once hatched, the adult flea must feed within a few days.

Once the adult flea finds a host, it will not leave voluntarily. It only becomes dislodged by grooming or the host animal's scratching. The adult flea will remain on the host for the duration of its life unless forcibly removed.

TREATING THE ENVIRONMENT AND THE DOG

Treating fleas should be a two-pronged attack. First, the environment needs to be treated; this includes carpets and furniture, especially the dog's bedding and areas underneath furniture. The environment should be treated with a household spray containing an Insect Growth Regulator (IGR) and an insecticide to kill the adult fleas. Most IGRs are effective against eggs and larvae; they actually mimic the fleas' own hormones and stop the eggs and larvae from developing into adult fleas. There are currently no treatments available to attack the pupa stage of the life cycle, so the adult insecticide is used to kill the newly hatched adult fleas before they find a host. Most IGRs are active for many months, while adult insecticides are only active

A scanning electron micrograph of a dog or cat flea, *Ctenocephalides,* magnified more than 100x. This image has been colorized for effect.

S. E. M. BY DR. DENNIS KUNKEL, UNIVERSITY OF HAWAII

THE LIFE CYCLE OF THE FLEA

Adult

Egg

**Pupa
or
Nymph**

Larva

Fleas have been around for millions of years and have adapted to changing host animals. They are able to go through a complete life cycle in less than one month or they can extend their lives to almost two years by remaining as pupae or cocoons. They do not need blood or any other food for up to 20 months.

IGR'S

Two types of products should be used when treating fleas—a product to treat the pet and a product to treat the home. Adult fleas represent less than 1% of the flea population. The pre-adult fleas (eggs, larvae and pupae) represent more than 99% of the flea population and are found in the environment; it is in the case of pre-adult fleas that products containing an Insect Growth Regulator (IGR) should be used in the home.

IGRs are a new class of compounds used to prevent the development of insects. They do not kill the insect outright, but instead use the insect's biology against it to stop it from completing its growth. Products that contain methoprene are the world's first and leading IGRs. Used to control fleas and other insects, this type of IGR will stop flea larvae from developing and protect the house for up to seven months.

The American dog tick, *Dermacentor variabilis*, is probably the most common tick found on dogs. Look at the strength in its eight legs! No wonder it's hard to detach them.

for a few days.

When treating with a household spray, it is a good idea to vacuum before applying the product. This stimulates as many pupae as possible to hatch into adult fleas. The vacuum cleaner should also be treated with an insecticide to prevent the eggs and larvae that have been collected in the vacuum bag from hatching.

The second stage of treatment is to apply an adult insecticide to the dog. Traditionally, this would be in the form of a collar or a spray, but more recent innovations include digestible insecticides that poison the fleas when they ingest the dog's blood. Alternatively, there are drops that, when placed on the back of the dog's neck, spread throughout the hair and skin to kill adult fleas.

Ticks

Though not as common as fleas, ticks are found all over the tropical and temperate world. They don't bite, like fleas; they harpoon. They dig their sharp proboscis (nose) into the dog's skin and drink the blood. Their only food and drink is dog's

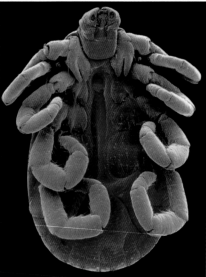

S. E. M. by Dr. Dennis Kunkel, University of Hawaii

blood. Dogs can get Lyme disease, Rocky Mountain spotted fever, tick bite paralysis and many other diseases from ticks. They may live where fleas are found and they like to hide in cracks or seams in walls. They are controlled the same way fleas are controlled.

The American dog tick, *Dermacentor variabilis*, may well be the most common dog tick in many geographical areas, especially those areas where the climate is hot and humid. Most dog ticks have life expectancies of a week to six months, depending upon climatic conditions. They can neither jump nor fly, but they can crawl slowly and can range up to 16 feet to reach a sleeping or unsuspecting dog.

MITES

Just as fleas and ticks can be problematic for your dog, mites can also lead to an itchy nuisance. Microscopic in size, mites are related to ticks and generally take up permanent residence on their host animal— in this case, your dog! The term *mange* refers to any infestation caused by one of the mighty mites, of which there are six varieties that concern dog owners.

Demodex mites cause a condition known as demodicosis (sometimes called red mange or follicular mange), in which the

DEER-TICK CROSSING

The great outdoors may be fun for your dog, but it also is a home to dangerous ticks. Deer ticks carry a bacterium known as *Borrelia burgdorferi* and are most active in the autumn and spring. When infections are caught early, penicillin and tetracycline are effective antibiotics, but, if left untreated, the bacteria may cause neurological, kidney and cardiac problems as well as long-term trouble with walking and painful joints.

The head of an American dog tick, *Dermacentor variabilis*, enlarged and colorized for effect.

123

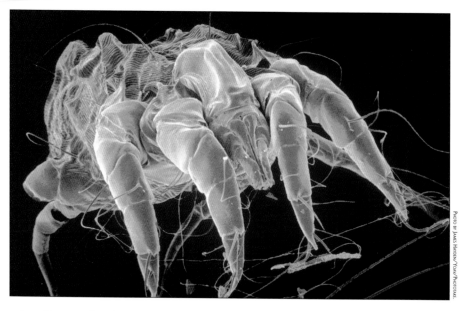

The mange mite, *Psoroptes bovis*, can infest cattle and other domestic animals.

PHOTO BY JAMES HAYDEN/YOAV/PHOTOTAKE

Human lice look like dog lice; the two are closely related.

PHOTO BY DWIGHT R. KUHN.

mites live in the dog's hair follicles and sebaceous glands in larger-than-normal numbers. This type of mange is commonly passed from the dam to her puppies and usually shows up on the puppies' muzzles, though demodicosis is not transferable from one normal dog to another. Most dogs recover from this type of mange without any treatment, though topical therapies are commonly prescribed by the vet.

The *Cheyletiellosis* mite is the hook-mouthed culprit associated with "walking dandruff," a condition that affects dogs as well as cats and rabbits. This mite lives on the surface of the animal's skin and is readily transferable through direct or indirect contact with an affected animal. The dandruff is present in the form of scaly skin, which may or may not be itchy. If not treated, this mange can affect a whole kennel of dogs and can be spread to humans as well.

The *Sarcoptes* mite causes intense itching on the dog in the form of a condition known as scabies or sarcoptic mange. The cycle of the *Sarcoptes* mite lasts about three weeks, and the mites live in the top layer of the dog's skin (epidermis), preferably in areas with little hair. Scabies is highly contagious and can be passed to humans. Sometimes an allergic reaction to the mite worsens the severe itching associated with sarcoptic mange.

Ear mites, *Otodectes cynotis,* lead to otodectic mange, which most commonly affects the outer ear canal of the dog, though other areas can be affected as well. Dogs with ear-mite infestation commonly scratch at their ears, causing further irritation, and shake their heads. Dark brown droppings in the outer ear confirm the diagnosis. Your vet can prescribe a treatment to flush out the ears and kill any eggs in the ears. A complete month of treatment is necessary to cure the mange.

Two other mites, less common in dogs, include *Dermanyssus gallinae* (the poultry or red mite) and *Eutrombicula alfreddugesi* (the North American mite associated with trombiculidiasis or chigger infestation). The poultry mite frequently lives on chickens, but can transfer to dogs who spend time near farm animals. Chigger infestation affects dogs in the Central US who have

NOT A DROP TO DRINK

Never allow your dog to swim in polluted water or public areas where water quality can be suspect. Even perfectly clear water can harbor parasites, many of which can cause serious to fatal illnesses in canines. Areas inhabited by waterfowl and other wildlife are especially dangerous.

DO NOT MIX

Never mix parasite-control products without first consulting your vet. Some products can become toxic when combined with others and can cause fatal consequences.

exposure to woodlands. The types of mange caused by both of these mites are treatable by vets.

INTERNAL PARASITES

Most animals—fishes, birds and mammals, including dogs and humans—have worms and other parasites that live inside their bodies. According to Dr. Herbert R. Axelrod, the fish pathologist, there are two kinds of parasites: dumb and smart. The smart parasites live in peaceful cooperation with their hosts (symbiosis), while the dumb parasites kill their hosts. Most worm infections are relatively easy to control. If they are not controlled, they weaken the host dog to the point that other medical problems occur, but they do not kill the host as dumb parasites would.

A brown dog tick, *Rhipicephalus sanguineus*, is an uncommon but annoying tick found on dogs.

125

The roundworm *Rhabditis* can infect both dogs and humans.

The roundworm, *Ascaris lumbricoides*.

ROUNDWORMS

Average-size dogs can pass 1,360,000 roundworm eggs every day. For example, if there were only 1 million dogs in the world, the world would be saturated with thousands of tons of dog feces. These feces would contain around 15,000,000,000 roundworm eggs.

Up to 31% of home yards and children's sand boxes in the US contain roundworm eggs.

Flushing dog's feces down the toilet is not a safe practice because the usual sewage treatments do not destroy roundworm eggs.

Infected puppies start shedding roundworm eggs at three weeks of age. They can be infected by their mother's milk.

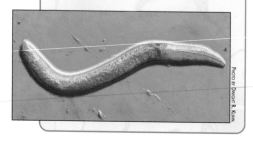

ROUNDWORMS

The roundworms that infect dogs are known scientifically as *Toxocara canis*. They live in the dog's intestines and shed eggs continually. It has been estimated that a dog produces about 6 or more ounces of feces every day. Each ounce of feces averages hundreds of thousands of roundworm eggs. There are no known areas in which dogs roam that do not contain roundworm eggs. The greatest danger of roundworms is that they infect people, too! It is wise to have your dog tested regularly for roundworms.

In young puppies, roundworms cause bloated bellies, diarrhea, coughing and vomiting, and are transmitted from the dam (through blood or milk). Affected puppies will not appear as animated as normal puppies. The worms appear spaghetti-like, measuring as long as 6 inches. Adult dogs can acquire roundworms through coprophagia (eating contaminated feces) or by killing rodents that carry roundworms.

Roundworm infection can kill puppies and cause severe problems in adults, as the hatched larvae travel to the lungs and trachea through the bloodstream. Cleanliness is the best preventative for roundworms. Always pick up after your dog and dispose of feces in appropriate receptacles.

HOOKWORMS

In the United States, dog owners have to be concerned about four different species of hookworm, the most common and most serious of which is *Ancylostoma caninum,* which prefers warm climates. The others are *Ancylostoma braziliense, Ancylostoma tubaeforme* and *Uncinaria stenocephala,* the latter of which is a concern to dogs living in the Northern US and Canada, as this species prefers cold climates. Hookworms are dangerous to humans as well as to dogs and cats, and can be the cause of severe anemia due to iron deficiency. The worm uses its teeth to attach itself to the dog's intestines and changes the site of its attachment about six times per day. Each time the worm repositions itself, the dog

loses blood and can become anemic. *Ancylostoma caninum* is the most likely of the four species to cause anemia in the dog.

Symptoms of hookworm infection include dark stools, weight loss, general weakness, pale coloration and anemia, as well as possible skin problems. Fortunately, hookworms are easily purged from the affected dog with a number of medications that have proven effective. Discuss these with your vet. Most heartworm preventatives include a hookworm insecticide as well.

Owners also must be aware that hookworms can infect humans, who can acquire the larvae through exposure to contaminated feces. Since the worms cannot complete their life cycle on a human, the worms simply infest the skin and cause irritation. This condition is known as cutaneous larva migrans syndrome. As a preventative, use disposable gloves or a "poop-scoop" to pick up your dog's droppings and prevent your dog (or neighborhood cats) from defecating in children's play areas.

The hookworm, *Ancylostoma caninum.*

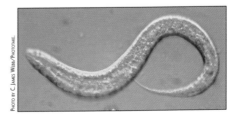

The infective stage of the hookworm larva.

127

TAPEWORMS

Humans, rats, squirrels, foxes, coyotes, wolves and domestic dogs are all susceptible to tapeworm infection. Except in humans, tapeworms are usually not a fatal infection. Infected individuals can harbor 1000 parasitic worms.

Tapeworms, like some other types of worm, are hermaphroditic, meaning male and female in the same worm.

If dogs eat infected rats or mice, or anything else infected with tapeworm, they get the tapeworm disease. One month after attaching to a dog's intestine, the worm starts shedding eggs. These eggs are infective immediately. Infective eggs can live for a few months without a host animal.

The head and rostellum (the round prominence on the scolex) of a tapeworm, which infects dogs and humans.

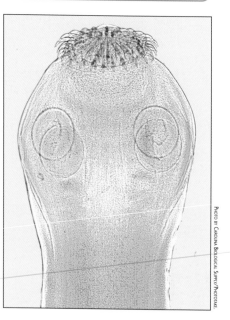

TAPEWORMS

There are many species of tapeworm, all of which are carried by fleas! The most common tapeworm affecting dogs is known as *Dipylidium caninum*. The dog eats the flea and starts the tapeworm cycle. Humans can also be infected with tapeworms—so don't eat fleas! Fleas are so small that your dog could pass them onto your hands, your plate or your food and thus make it possible for you to ingest a flea that is carrying tapeworm eggs.

While tapeworm infection is not life-threatening in dogs (smart parasite!), it can be the cause of a very serious liver disease for humans. About 50% of the humans infected with *Echinococcus multilocularis*, a type of tapeworm that causes alveolar hydatid, perish.

WHIPWORMS

In North America, whipworms are counted among the most common parasitic worms in dogs. The whipworm's scientific name is *Trichuris vulpis*. These worms attach themselves in the lower parts of the intestine, where they feed. Affected dogs may only experience upset tummies, colic and diarrhea. These worms, however, can live for months or years in the dog, beginning their larval stage in the small intestine, spending their adult stage in the large intestine and finally passing infective eggs through the dog's feces. The only way to detect whipworms is through a fecal examination, though this is not always foolproof. Treatment for whipworms is tricky, due to the worms' unusual life-cycle pattern, and very often dogs are reinfected due to exposure to infective eggs on the ground. The whipworm eggs can survive in the environment for as long as five years; thus, cleaning up droppings in your own backyard as well as in public places is absolutely essential for sanitation purposes and the health of your dog and others.

THREADWORMS

Though less common than roundworms, hookworms and those previously mentioned, threadworms concern dog owners in the Southwestern US and Gulf Coast area where the climate is hot and humid. Living in the small intestine of the dog, this worm measures a mere 2 millimeters and is round in shape. Like that of the whipworm, the threadworm's life cycle is very complex and the eggs and larvae are passed through the feces. A deadly disease in humans, *Strongyloides* readily infects people, and the handling of feces is the most common means of transmission. Threadworms are most often seen in young puppies; bloody diarrhea and pneumonia are symptoms. Sick puppies must be isolated and treated immediately; vets recommend a follow-up treatment one month later.

HEARTWORM PREVENTATIVES

There are many heartworm preventatives on the market, many of which are sold at your veterinarian's office. These products can be given daily or monthly, depending on the manufacturer's instructions. All of these preventatives contain chemical insecticides directed at killing heartworms, which leads to some controversy among dog owners. In effect, heartworm preventatives are necessary evils, though you should determine how necessary based on your pet's lifestyle. There is no doubt that heartworm is a dreadful disease that threatens the lives of dogs. However, the likelihood of your dog's being bitten by an infected mosquito is slim in most places, and a mosquito-repellent (or an herbal remedy such as Wormwood or Black Walnut) is much safer for your dog and will not compromise his immune system (the way heartworm preventatives will). Should you decide to use the traditional preventative "medications," you can consider giving the pill every other or third month. Since the toxins in the pill will kill the heartworms at all stages of development, the pill would be effective in killing larvae, nymphs or adults, and it takes four months for the larvae to reach the adult stage. Thus, there is no rationale to poisoning the dog's system on a monthly basis. Lastly, do not give the pill during the winter months, since there are no mosquitoes around to pass on their infection, unless you live in a tropical environment.

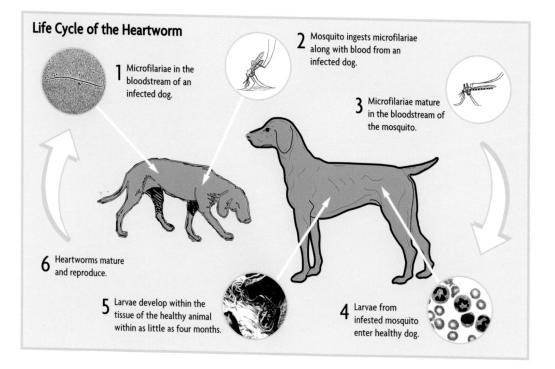

Life Cycle of the Heartworm

1 Microfilariae in the bloodstream of an infected dog.

2 Mosquito ingests microfilariae along with blood from an infected dog.

3 Microfilariae mature in the bloodstream of the mosquito.

6 Heartworms mature and reproduce.

5 Larvae develop within the tissue of the healthy animal within as little as four months.

4 Larvae from infested mosquito enter healthy dog.

HEARTWORMS

Heartworms are thin, extended worms up to 12 inches long, which live in a dog's heart and the major blood vessels surrounding it. Dogs may have up to 200 worms. Symptoms may be loss of energy, loss of appetite, coughing, the development of a pot belly and anemia.

Heartworms are transmitted by mosquitoes. The mosquito drinks the blood of an infected dog and takes in larvae with the blood. The larvae, called microfilariae, develop within the body of the mosquito and are passed on to the next dog bitten after the larvae mature. It takes two to three weeks for the larvae to develop to the infective stage within the body of the mosquito. Dogs are usually treated at about six weeks of age and maintained on a prophylactic dose given monthly.

Blood testing for heartworms is not necessarily indicative of how seriously your dog is infected. Although this is a dangerous disease, it is not easy for a dog to be infected. Discuss the various preventatives with your vet, as there are many different types now available. Together you can decide on a safe course of prevention for your dog.

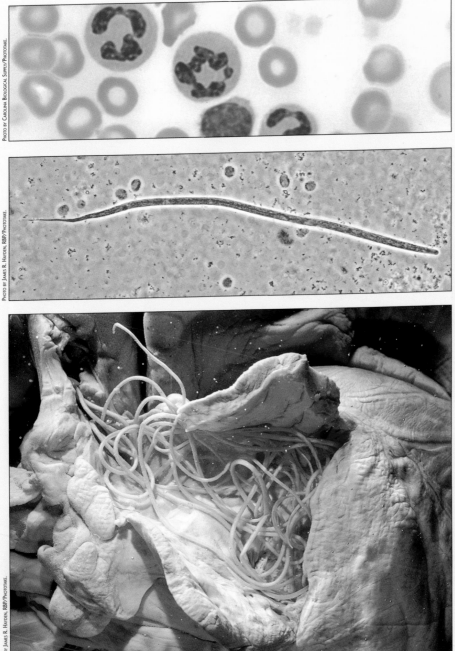

Photo by Carolina Biological Supply/Phototake.

Magnified heartworm larvae, *Dirofilaria immitis.*

Photo by James R. Hayden, RBP/Phototake.

Heartworm, *Dirofilaria immitis.*

The heart of a dog infected with canine heartworm, *Dirofilaria immitis.*

Photo by James R. Hayden, RBP/Phototake.

HOMEOPATHY:
an alternative to conventional medicine

"Less is Most"

Using this principle, the strength of a homeopathic remedy is measured by the number of serial dilutions that were undertaken to create it. The greater the number of serial dilutions, the greater the strength of the homeopathic remedy. The potency of a remedy that has been made by making a dilution of 1 part in 100 parts (or 1/100) is 1c or 1cH. If this remedy is subjected to a series of further dilutions, each one being 1/100, a more dilute and stronger remedy is produced. If the remedy is diluted in this way six times, it is called 6c or 6cH. A dilution of 6c is 1 part in 1,000,000,000,000. In general, higher potencies in more frequent doses are better for acute symptoms and lower potencies in more infrequent doses are more useful for chronic, long-standing problems.

CURING OUR DOGS NATURALLY

Holistic medicine means treating the whole animal as a unique, perfect living being. Generally, holistic treatments do not suppress the symptoms that the body naturally produces, as do most medications prescribed by conventional doctors and vets. Holistic methods seek to cure disease by regaining balance and harmony in the patient's environment. Some of these methods include use of nutritional therapy, herbs, flower essences, aromatherapy, acupuncture, massage, chiropractic and, of course, the most popular holistic approach, homeopathy.

Homeopathy is a theory or system of treating illness with small doses of substances which, if administered in larger quantities, would produce the symptoms that the patient already has. This approach is often described as "like cures like." Although modern veterinary medicine is geared toward the "quick fix," homeopathy relies on the belief that, given the time, the body is able to heal itself and return to its natural, healthy state.

Choosing a remedy to cure a problem in our dogs is the difficult part of homeopathy. Consult with your veterinarian for a professional diagnosis of your dog's symptoms. Often these symptoms require immediate conventional care. If your vet is willing and knowledgeable, you may attempt a homeopathic remedy. Be aware that cortisone prevents homeopathic remedies from working. There are hundreds of possibilities and combinations to cure many problems in dogs, from basic physical problems such as excessive shedding, fleas or other parasites, unattractive doggy odor, bad breath, upset tummy, obesity, dry, oily or dull coat, diarrhea, ear problems or eye discharge (including tears and dry or mucousy matter), to behavioural abnormalities such as fear of loud noises, habitual licking, poor appetite, excessive barking and various phobias. From alumina to zincum metallicum, the remedies span the planet and the imagination…from flowers and weeds to chemicals, insect droppings, diesel smoke and volcanic ash.

Using "Like to Treat Like"

Unlike conventional medicines that suppress symptoms, homeopathic remedies treat illnesses with small doses of substances that, if administered in larger quantities, would produce the symptoms that the patient already has. While the same homeopathic remedy can be used to treat different symptoms in different dogs, here are some interesting remedies and their uses.

Apis Mellifica
(made from honey bee venom) can be used for allergies or to reduce swelling that occurs in acutely infected kidneys.

Diesel Smoke
can be used to help control motion sickness.

Calcarea Fluorica
(made from calcium fluoride, which helps harden bone structure) can be useful in treating hard lumps in tissues.

Natrum Muriaticum
(made from common salt, sodium chloride) is useful in treating thin, thirsty dogs.

Nitricum Acidum
(made from nitric acid) is used for symptoms you would expect to see from contact with acids such as lesions, especially where the skin joins the linings of body orifices or openings such as the lips and nostrils.

Symphytum
(made from the herb Knitbone, *Symphytum officianale*) is used to encourage bones to heal.

Urtica Urens
(made from the common stinging nettle) is used in treating painful, irritating rashes.

HOMEOPATHIC REMEDIES FOR YOUR DOG

Symptom/Ailment	Possible Remedy
ALLERGIES	Apis Mellifica 30c, Astacus Fluviatilis 6c, Pulsatilla 30c, Urtica Urens 6c
ALOPECIA	Alumina 30c, Lycopodium 30c, Sepia 30c, Thallium 6c
ANAL GLANDS (BLOCKED)	Hepar Sulphuris Calcareum 30c, Sanicula 6c, Silicea 6c
ARTHRITIS	Rhus Toxicodendron 6c, Bryonia Alba 6c
CANINE COUGH	Drosera 6c, Ipecacuanha 30c
CATARACT	Calcarea Carbonica 6c, Conium Maculatum 6c, Phosphorus 30c, Silicea 30c
CONSTIPATION	Alumina 6c, Carbo Vegetabilis 30c, Graphites 6c, Nitricum Acidum 30c, Silicea 6c
COUGHING	Aconitum Napellus 6c, Belladonna 30c, Hyoscyamus Niger 30c, Phosphorus 30c
DIARRHEA	Arsenicum Album 30c, Aconitum Napellus 6c, Chamomilla 30c, Mercurius Corrosivus 30c
DRY EYE	Zincum Metallicum 30c
EAR PROBLEMS	Aconitum Napellus 30c, Belladonna 30c, Hepar Sulphuris 30c, Tellurium 30c, Psorinum 200c
EYE PROBLEMS	Borax 6c, Aconitum Napellus 30c, Graphites 6c, Staphysagria 6c, Thuja Occidentalis 30c
GLAUCOMA	Aconitum Napellus 30c, Apis Mellifica 6c, Phosphorus 30c
HEAT STROKE	Belladonna 30c, Gelsemium Sempervirens 30c, Sulphur 30c
HICCOUGHS	Cinchona Deficinalis 6c
HIP DYSPLASIA	Colocynthis 6c, Rhus Toxicodendron 6c, Bryonia Alba 6c
INCONTINENCE	Argentum Nitricum 6c, Causticum 30c, Conium Maculatum 30c, Pulsatilla 30c, Sepia 30c
INSECT BITES	Apis Mellifica 30c, Cantharis 30c, Hypericum Perforatum 6c, Urtica Urens 30c
ITCHING	Alumina 30c, Arsenicum Album 30c, Carbo Vegetabilis 30c, Hypericum Perforatum 6c, Mezerium 6c, Sulphur 30c
MASTITIS	Apis Mellifica 30c, Belladonna 30c, Urtica Urens 1m
MOTION SICKNESS	Cocculus 6c, Petroleum 6c
PATELLAR LUXATION	Gelsemium Sempervirens 6c, Rhus Toxicodendron 6c
PENIS PROBLEMS	Aconitum Napellus 30c, Hepar Sulphuris Calcareum 30c, Pulsatilla 30c, Thuja Occidentalis 6c
PUPPY TEETHING	Calcarea Carbonica 6c, Chamomilla 6c, Phytolacca 6c

CDS: COGNITIVE DYSFUNCTION SYNDROME
"OLD-DOG SYNDROME"

There are many ways for you to evaluate old-dog syndrome. Veterinarians have defined CDS (cognitive dysfunction syndrome) as the gradual deterioration of cognitive abilities. These are indicated by changes in the dog's behavior. When a dog changes his routine response, and maladies have been eliminated as the cause of these behavioral changes, then CDS is the usual diagnosis.

More than half the dogs over eight years old suffer from some form of CDS. The older the dog, the more chance it has of suffering from CDS. In humans, doctors often dismiss the CDS behavioral changes as part of "winding down."

There are four major signs of CDS: frequent potty accidents inside the home, sleeping much more or much less than normal, acting confused and failure to respond to social stimuli.

SYMPTOMS OF CDS

FREQUENT POTTY ACCIDENTS
- *Urinates in the house.*
- *Defecates in the house.*
- *Doesn't signal that he wants to go out.*

SLEEP PATTERNS
- *Awakens more slowly.*
- *Sleeps more than normal during the day.*
- *Sleeps less during the night.*

CONFUSION
- *Walks around listlessly and without a destination goal.*
- *Goes outside and just stands there.*
- *Appears confused with a faraway look in his eyes.*
- *Hides more often.*
- *Doesn't recognize friends.*
- *Doesn't come when called.*

FAILURE TO RESPOND TO SOCIAL STIMULI
- *Comes to people less frequently, whether called or not.*
- *Doesn't tolerate petting for more than a short time.*
- *Doesn't come to the door when you return home from work.*

The term *old* is a qualitative term. For dogs, as well as their masters, old is relative. Certainly we can all distinguish between a puppy Beagle and an adult Beagle—there are the obvious physical traits, such as size, appearance and facial expressions, as well as personality traits. Puppies and young dogs like to play with children. Children's natural exuberance is a good match for the seemingly endless energy of young dogs. They like to run, jump, chase and retrieve. When dogs grow up and cease their interaction with children, they are often thought of as being too old to play with the kids. On the other hand, if a Beagle is only exposed to people with quieter lifestyles, his life will normally be less active and the decrease in his activity level as he ages will not be as obvious.

If people live to be 100 years old, dogs live to be 20 years old. While this is a good rule of thumb, it is very inaccurate. When trying to compare dog years to human years, you cannot make a generalization about all dogs. You can make the generalization that 12 years is a good lifespan for a Beagle, which is quite good compared to many other purebred

A sure sign of old age in a Beagle is the loss of color on the muzzle.

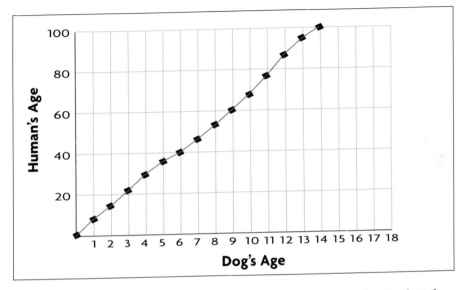

dogs that may only live to 8 or 9 years of age. Some Beagles have been known to live to 15 years.

Dogs are generally considered mature within three years, but they can reproduce even earlier. So the first three years of a dog's life are like seven times that of comparable humans. That means a 3-year-old dog is like a 21-year-old human. But, as the curve of comparison shows, there is no hard and fast rule for comparing dog and human ages. The comparison is made even more difficult, for not all humans age at the same rate...and human females live longer than human males.

CARING FOR A SENIOR
Most veterinarians and behaviorists use the seven-year mark as the time to consider a dog a "senior."

This term does not imply that the dog is geriatric and has begun to fail in mind and body. Aging is essentially a slowing process. Humans readily admit that they feel a difference in their activity level from age 20 to 30, and then from 30 to 40, etc. By treating the seven-year-old dog as a senior, owners are able to implement certain therapeutic and preventative medical strategies with the help of their veterinarians.

A special-care program should include at least two veterinary visits per year and screening sessions to determine the dog's health status, as well as nutritional counseling. Veterinarians determine the senior dog's health status through a blood smear for a complete blood count, serum chemistry profile with electrolytes, urinalysis, blood pressure check, electrocardiogram, ocular tonometry (pressure on the eyeball) and dental prophylaxis.

Such an extensive program for senior dogs is well advised before owners start to see the obvious physical signs of aging, such as slower and inhibited movement, graying, increased sleep/nap periods and disinterest in play and other activity. This preventative program promises a longer, healthier life for the aging dog. Among the physical problems common in aging dogs are the loss of sight and hearing, arthritis, kidney and liver failure, diabetes mellitus, heart disease and Cushing's disease (a hormonal disease).

SENIOR SIGNS

An old dog starts to show one or more of the following symptoms:
- The hair on the face and paws starts to turn gray. The color breakdown usually starts around the eyes and mouth.
- Sleep patterns are deeper and longer, and the old dog is harder to awaken.
- Food intake diminishes.
- Responses to calls, whistles and other signals are ignored more and more.
- Eye contact does not evoke tail wagging (assuming it once did).

In addition to the physical manifestations discussed, there are some behavioral changes and problems related to aging dogs. Dogs suffering from hearing or vision loss, dental discomfort or arthritis can become aggressive. Likewise, the near-deaf and/or blind dog may be startled more easily and react in an unexpectedly aggressive manner. Seniors suffering from senility can become more impatient and irritable. Housesoiling accidents are associated with loss of mobility, kidney problems and loss of sphincter control as well as plaque accumulation, physiological brain changes and reactions to medications. Older dogs, just like young puppies, suffer from separation anxiety, which can lead to excessive barking, whining, housesoiling and destructive behavior. Seniors may become fearful of everyday sounds, such as vacuum cleaners, heaters, thunder and passing traffic. Some dogs have difficulty sleeping, due to discomfort, the need for frequent toilet visits and the like.

Owners should avoid spoiling the older dog with too many fatty treats. Obesity is a common problem in older dogs and subtracts years from their lives. Keep the senior dog as trim as possible since excessive weight puts additional stress on the body's vital organs. Some breeders recommend supplementing the diet with foods high in fiber and lower in calories. Adding fresh vegetables and marrow broth to the senior's diet makes a tasty, low-calorie, low-fat supplement. Vets also offer specialty diets for senior dogs that are worth exploring.

Your dog, as he nears his twilight years, needs his owner's patience and good care more than ever. Never punish an older dog for an accident or abnormal behavior. For all the years of love, protection and companionship that your dog has provided, he deserves special attention and courtesies. The older dog may need to relieve himself at 3 a.m. because he can no longer hold it for eight hours. Older dogs may not be able to remain crated for more than two or three hours. It may be time to give up a sofa or chair to your old friend. Although he may not seem as enthusiastic about your attention and petting, he does appreciate the considerations you offer as he gets older.

Your Beagle does not understand why his world is slowing down. Owners must make the transition into the golden years as pleasant and rewarding as possible.

WHEN THE TIME COMES

You are never fully prepared to make a rational decision about putting your dog to sleep. It is very obvious that you love your Beagle or you would not be reading this book. Putting a loved dog to sleep is extremely difficult. It is a decision that must be made with your veterinarian. You are usually forced to make the decision when your dog experiences life-threatening symptoms that become serious enough for you to seek medical (veterinary) help.

If the prognosis of the malady indicates the end is near and your beloved pet will only suffer

NOTICING SYMPTOMS

The symptoms listed below are symptoms that gradually appear and become more noticeable. They are not life-threatening; however, the symptoms below are to be taken very seriously and warrant a discussion with your veterinarian:

• Your dog cries and whimpers when he moves, and he stops running completely.

• Convulsions start or become more serious and frequent. The usual convulsion (spasm) is when the dog stiffens and starts to tremble, being unable or unwilling to move. The seizure usually lasts for 5 to 30 minutes.

• Your dog drinks more water and urinates more frequently. Wetting and bowel accidents take place indoors without warning.

• Vomiting becomes more and more frequent.

Dogs can be buried in pet cemeteries. Your vet can advise you about the location of a pet cemetery near your home.

more and experience no enjoyment for the balance of his life, then euthanasia is the right choice.

WHAT IS EUTHANASIA?
Euthanasia derives from the Greek, meaning *good death*. In other words, it means the planned, painless killing of a dog suffering from a painful, incurable condition, or who is so aged that he cannot walk, see, eat or control his excretory functions.

Euthanasia is usually accomplished by injection with an overdose of an anesthesia or barbiturate. Aside from the prick of the needle, the experience is usually painless.

The decision to euthanize your dog is never easy. The days during which the dog becomes ill and the end occurs can be unusually stressful for you. If this is your first experience with the death of a loved one, you may need the comfort dictated by your religious beliefs. If you are the head of the family and have children, you should have involved them in the decision of putting your Beagle to sleep. Usually your dog can be maintained on drugs for a few days in order to give you ample time to make a decision. During this time, talking with members of your family or even people who have lived through this same experience can ease the burden of your inevitable decision.

THE FINAL RESTING PLACE
Dogs can have some of the same privileges as humans. They can occasionally be buried in a pet cemetery, which is generally

EUTHANASIA

Euthanasia is a procedure that must be performed by a licensed veterinarian. There also may be societies for the prevention of cruelty to animals in your area. They will often offer this service upon a veterinarian's recommendation.

COPING WITH LOSS

When your dog dies, you may be as upset as when a human companion passes away. You are losing your protector, your baby, your confidante and your best friend. Many people experience not only grief but also feelings of guilt and doubt as to whether they did all that they could for their pet. Allow yourself to grieve and mourn, and seek help from friends and support groups.

be afraid to ask financial questions. Cremations can be individual, but a less expensive option is mass cremation, although of course the ashes cannot then be returned. Vets can usually arrange cremation services on your behalf or can help you locate a pet cemetery.

GETTING ANOTHER DOG?

The grief of losing your beloved dog will be as lasting as the grief of losing a human friend or relative. In most cases, if your dog died of old age, it had slowed down considerably. Do you want a new Beagle puppy to replace it? Or are you better off in finding a more mature Beagle, say two to three years of age, which will usually be house-trained and will have an already developed personality. In this case, you can find out if you like each other after a few hours of being together.

The decision is, of course, your own. Do you want another Beagle or perhaps a different breed so as to avoid comparison with your beloved friend? Most people usually buy the same breed because they know (and love) the characteristics of that breed. Then, too, they often know people who have the same breed and perhaps they are lucky enough that a breeder they know and respect expects a litter soon. What could be better?

expensive, or, if they have died at home, can be buried in your yard in a place suitably marked with some stone or newly planted tree or bush. Alternatively, your dog can be cremated and the ashes returned to you, or some people prefer to leave their dogs with the veterinarian.

All of these options should be discussed frankly and openly with your veterinarian. Do not

Dogs can be cremated. Their ashes can be deposited in a suitable cemetery facility such as that shown here.

141

When you purchase your Beagle, you will make it clear to the breeder whether you want one just as a lovable companion and pet, or if you hope to be buying a Beagle with show prospects. No reputable breeder will sell you a young puppy and tell you that it is *definitely* of show quality, for so much can go wrong during the early months of a puppy's development. If you plan to show, what you will hopefully have acquired is a puppy with "show potential."

To the novice, exhibiting a Beagle in the show ring may look easy, but it takes a lot of hard work and devotion to do top winning at a show such as the prestigious Westminster Kennel Club dog show, not to mention a little luck too!

AKC GROUPS

For showing purposes, the AKC divides its recognized breeds into seven groups: Sporting Dogs, Hounds, Working Dogs, Terriers, Toys, Non-Sporting Dogs and Herding Dogs. The Miscellaneous Class comprises developing breeds awaiting full AKC recognition.

The first concept that the canine novice learns when watching a dog show is that each dog first competes against members of its own breed. Once the judge has selected the best member of each breed (Best of Breed), provided that the show is judged on a Group system, that chosen dog will compete with other Best of Breed dogs in its group. Finally, the dogs chosen first in each group will compete for Best in Show.

The second concept that you must understand is that the dogs are not actually compared against one another. The judge compares each dog against its breed standard, the written description of the ideal specimen that is approved by the American Kennel Club (AKC). Breeders attempt to get as close to this ideal as possible with every litter, but theoretically the "perfect" dog is so elusive that it is impossible. (And if the "perfect" dog were born, breeders and judges would never agree that it was indeed "perfect.")

If you are interested in exploring the world of dog showing, your best bet is to join your local breed club or the national parent club, which is the National Beagle Club. These clubs often host both regional and national specialties, shows only for Beagles, which can include conformation as well as obedience and field trials. Even if you have no intention of competing with your Beagle, a specialty is like a festival for lovers of the breed who congregate to share their favorite topic: Beagles! Clubs also send out newsletters, and some organize training days and seminars in order that people may learn more about their chosen breed. To locate the breed club closest to you, contact the American Kennel Club, which furnishes the rules and regulations for all of these events plus general dog registration and other basic requirements

With hard work, a great Beagle and lots of luck, you can win a show and get lovely medals, ribbons and full bragging rights.

MEET THE AKC

The American Kennel Club is the main governing body of the dog sport in the United States. Founded in 1884, the AKC consists of 500 or more independent dog clubs plus 4,500 affiliate clubs, all of which follow the AKC rules and regulations. Additionally, the AKC registers pure-bred dogs in the US and works to preserve the integrity of the sport and its continuation in the country. Over 1,000,000 dogs are registered each year, representing about 150 recognized breeds.

of dog ownership.

In the US, the American Kennel Club offers three kinds of conformation shows: An all-breed show (for all AKC-recognized breeds); a specialty show (for one breed only, usually sponsored by the parent club) and a Group show (for all breeds in the Group).

For a dog to become an AKC champion of record, the dog must accumulate 15 points at shows from at least three different judges, including two "majors." A

Many owners enjoy having a Beagle who is both a treasured companion and a success in the show ring.

"major" is defined as a three-, four- or five-point win, and the number of points per win is determined by the number of dogs entered in the show on that given day. Depending on the breed, the number of points that are awarded varies. In a breed as popular as the Beagle, more dogs are needed to rack up the points. At any dog show, only one dog and one bitch of each breed can win points.

The judge at the show begins judging the Puppy Class, first dogs and then bitches, and proceeds through the classes. The judge places his winners first through fourth in each class. In the Winners Class, the first-place winners of each class compete with one another to determine Winners Dog and Winners Bitch.

CLUB INFORMATION

You can get information about dog shows from the national kennel clubs:

American Kennel Club
5580 Centerview Dr., Raleigh, NC 27606-3390
www.akc.org

United Kennel Club
100 E. Kilgore Road, Kalamazoo, MI 49002
www.ukcdogs.com

Canadian Kennel Club
89 Skyway Ave., Suite 100, Etobicoke, Ontario
M9W 6R4 Canada
www.ckc.ca

The Kennel Club
1-5 Clarges St., Piccadilly, London W1Y 8AB, UK
www.the-kennel-club.org.uk

SHOW RING ETIQUETTE

Just as with anything else, there is a certain etiquette to the show ring that can only be learned through experience. Showing your dog can be quite intimidating to you as a novice when it seems as if everyone else knows what he is doing. You can familiarize yourself with ring procedure beforehand by taking handling classes to prepare you and your dog for conformation showing and by talking with experienced handlers. When you are in the ring, it is very important to pay attention and listen to the instructions you are given by the judge about where to move your dog. Remember, even the most skilled handlers had to start somewhere. Keep it up and you too will become a proficient handler as you gain practice and experience.

The judge also places a Reserve Winners Dog and Reserve Winners Bitch, which could be awarded the points in the case of a disqualification. The Winners Dog and Winners Bitch are the two that are awarded the points for the breed, then compete with any champions of record entered in the show. The judge reviews the Winners Dog, Winners Bitch and all the other champions to select his Best of Breed. The Best of Winners is selected between the Winners Dog and Winners

Bitch. Were one of these two to be selected Best of Breed, it would automatically be named Best of Winners as well. Finally the judge selects his Best of Opposite Sex to the Best of Breed winner.

At a Group show or all-breed

Here a handler and Beagle await evaluation by the judge.

show, the Best of Breed winners from each breed then compete against one another for Group One through Group Four. The judge compares each Best of Breed to its breed standard, and the dog that most closely lives up to the ideal for its breed is selected as Group One. Finally, all seven group winners (from the Hound Group, Sporting Group, Toy Group, etc.) compete for Best in Show.

To find out about dog shows in your area, you can subscribe to the American Kennel Club's monthly magazine, The *American Kennel Gazette* and the accompa-

nying Events Calendar. You can also look in your local newspaper for advertisements for dog shows in your area or go on the Internet to the AKC's website, www.akc.org.

If your Beagle is six months of age or older and registered with the AKC, you can enter him in a dog show where the breed is offered classes. Provided that your Beagle does not have a disqualifying fault, he can compete. Only unaltered dogs can be entered in a dog show, so if you have spayed or neutered your Beagle, you cannot compete in conformation shows. The reason for this is simple. Dog shows are the main forum to prove which representatives in a breed are worthy of being bred. Only dogs that have achieved championships—the AKC "seal of approval" for quality in purebred dogs—should be bred. Altered dogs, however, can participate in other AKC events such as obedience trials and the Canine Good Citizen® program.

Before you actually step into the ring, you would be well advised to sit back and observe the judge's ring procedure. The judge asks each handler to "stack" the dog, hopefully showing the dog off to his best advantage. The judge will observe the dog from a distance and from different angles, and approach the dog to check his teeth, overall

FIVE CLASSES AT SHOWS

At most AKC all-breed shows, there are five regular classes: Puppy, Novice, Bred-by-Exhibitor, American-bred and Open. The Puppy Class is usually divided as 6 to 9 and 9 to 12 months of age. When deciding in which class to enter your dog, male or female, you must carefully check the show schedule to make sure that you have selected the right class. Depending on the dog's age, previous first-place wins and sex, you must make the best choice. It is possible to enter a one-year-old dog who has not won sufficient first places in any of the non-Puppy Classes, though the competition is more intense.

Beagles are agile dogs and can usually compete very well in working, obedience and agility trials.

structure, alertness and muscle tone, as well as consider how well the dog "conforms" to the standard. Most importantly, the judge will have the exhibitor move the dog around the ring in some pattern that he should specify. Finally, the judge will give the dog one last look before moving on to the next exhibitor.

If you are not in the top four in your class at your first show, do not be discouraged. Be patient and you may eventually find yourself in a winning line-up. Remember that the winners have devoted many hours and much money to earn the placement. If you find that your dog is losing every time and never getting a nod, it may be time to consider a

CANINE GOOD CITIZEN®

Have you ever considered getting your dog "certified"? The AKC's Canine Good Citizen® Program affords your dog just that opportunity. Your dog shows he is a well-behaved canine citizen, by taking a series of ten tests that illustrate that he can behave properly at home, in a public place and around other dogs. The tests are administered by participating dog clubs, colleges, 4-H clubs, scouts and other community groups and are open to all purebred and mixed-breed dogs. Upon passing the ten tests, the suffix CGC is applied to your dog's name.

147

different dog sport or to just enjoy your Beagle as a pet. Parent clubs offer other events, such as agility, tracking, obedience, instinct tests and more, which may be of interest to the owner of a well-trained Beagle.

OBEDIENCE TRIALS

Obedience trials in the US trace back to the early 1930s when organized obedience training was developed to demonstrate how well dog and owner could work together. The pioneer of obedience trials is Mrs. Helen Whitehouse Walker, a Standard Poodle fancier, who designed a series of exercises after the Associated Sheep, Police Army Dog Society of Great Britain. Since the days of Mrs. Walker,

obedience trials have grown by leaps and bounds, and today there are over 2,000 trials held in the US every year, with more than 100,000 dogs competing. Any AKC-registered dog can enter an obedience trial, regardless of conformational disqualifications or neutering.

Obedience trials are divided into three levels of progressive difficulty. At the first level, the Novice, dogs compete for the title Companion Dog (CD); at the intermediate level, the Open, dogs compete for the title Companion Dog Excellent (CDX); and at the advanced level, dogs compete for the title Utility Dog (UD). Classes are sub-divided into "A" (for beginners) and "B" (for more experienced handlers). A perfect score at any level is 200, and a dog must score 170 or better to earn a "leg," of which three are needed to earn the title. To earn points, the dog must score more than 50% of the available points in each exercise.

Once a dog has earned the UD title, he can compete with other proven obedience dogs for the coveted title of Utility Dog Excellent (UDX), which requires that the dog win "legs" in ten shows. Utility Dogs who earn "legs" in Open B and Utility B earn points toward their Obedience Trial Champion title. To become an OTCh., a dog needs to earn 100 points, which

JR. SHOWMANSHIP

For budding dog handlers, ages 10 to 18 years, Junior Showmanship competitions are an excellent training ground for the next generation of dog professionals. Junior handlers learn by grooming, handling and training their dogs, and the quality of junior's presentation of the dog (and himself) is being evaluated by a licensed judge. The junior can enter with any AKC-registered dog to compete, provided that the dog lives with him or a member of his family.

requires three first places in Open B and Utility under three different judges.

The Grand Prix of obedience trials, the AKC National

TEMPERAMENT PLUS

Although it seems that physical conformation is the only factor considered in the show ring, temperament is also of utmost importance. An aggressive or fearful dog should not be shown, as bad behavior will not be tolerated and may pose a threat to the judge, other exhibitors, you and your dog.

Obedience Invitational gives qualifying Utility Dogs the chance to win the newest and highest title: National Obedience Champion (NOC). Only the top 25 ranked obedience dogs, plus any dog ranked in the top 3 in its breed, are allowed to compete.

AGILITY TRIALS

Having had its origins in the UK back in 1977, AKC agility had its official beginning in the US in August 1994, when the first licensed agility trials were held. The AKC allows all registered breeds (including Miscellaneous Class breeds) to participate,

Foxhounds and Beagles participate in demonstrations, working with the hunters and horses. The red coats are traditional apparel for these hound spectacles.

149

The most prestigious dog show in the United States takes place in New York City. The Westminster Kennel Club Show attracts the finest dogs in the country to compete.

NO SHOW

Never show a dog that is sick or recovering from surgery or infection. Not only will this put your own dog under a tremendous amount of stress, but you will also put other dogs at risk of contracting any illness your dog has. Likewise, bitches who are in heat will distract and disrupt the performances of males who are competing, and bitches that are pregnant will likely be stressed and exhausted by a long day of showing.

providing the dog is 12 months of age or older. Agility is designed so that the handler demonstrates how well the dog can work at his side. The handler directs his dog over an obstacle course that includes jumps as well as tires, the dog walk, weave poles, pipe tunnels, collapsed tunnels, etc. While working their way through the course, the dog must keep one eye and ear on the handler and the rest of his body on the course. The handler gives verbal and hand signals to guide the dog through the course.

The first organization to promote agility trials in the US was the United States Dog Agility Association, Inc. (USDAA), which was established in 1986 and spawned numerous member clubs around the country. Both the

USDAA and the AKC offer titles to winning dogs.

Agility is great fun for dog and owner with many rewards for everyone involved. Interested owners should join a training club that has obstacles and experienced agility handlers who can introduce you and your dog to the "ropes" (and tires, tunnels, etc.).

TRACKING

Tracking tests are exciting and competitive ways to test your Beagle's extraordinary nose and scenting ability. The AKC started tracking tests in 1937, when the first AKC-licensed test took place as part of the Utility level at an obedience trial. Ten years later in 1947, the AKC offered the first title, Tracking Dog (TD). It was not until 1980 that the AKC added the Tracking Dog Excellent title (TDX), which was followed by the Versatile Surface Tracking title (VST) in

1995. The title Champion Tracker (CT) is awarded to a dog who has earned all three titles

FIELD TRIALS

Field trials are offered to the retrievers, pointers and spaniel breeds of the Sporting Group as well as to the Beagles, Dachshunds and Bassets of the Hound Group. The purpose of field trials is to demonstrate a dog's ability to perform its original purpose in the field. The events vary depending on the type of dog, but in all trials dogs compete against one another for placement and for points toward their Field Champion (FC) titles.

Every field trial includes four stakes of increasing levels of difficulty. Each stake is judged by a team of two judges who look for many natural abilities, including steadiness, courage, style, control and training.

During an agility trial, the Beagle easily maneuvers his way through the weave poles.

GLOSSARY

This glossary is intended to help you, the Beagle owner, better understand the specific terms used in this book as well as other terms that might surface in discussions with your veterinarian during his care of your Beagle.

Abscess a pus-filled inflamed area of body tissue.

Acral lick granuloma unexplained licking of an area, usually the leg, that prevents healing of original wound.

Acute disease a disease whose onset is sudden and fast.

Albino an animal totally lacking in pigment (always white).

Allergy a known sensitivity that results from exposure to a given allergen.

Alopecia lack of hair.

Amaurosis an unexplained blindness from the retina.

Anemia red-blood-cell deficiency.

Arthritis joint inflammation.

Atopic dermatitis congenital-allergen-caused inflammation of the skin.

Atrophy wasting away caused by faulty nutrition; a reduction in size.

Bloat see gastric dilatation.

Calculi mineral "stone" located in a vital organ, i.e., gall bladder.

Cancer a tumor that continues to expand and grow rapidly.

Carcinoma cancerous growth in the skin.

Cardiac arrhythmia irregular heartbeat.

Cardiomyopathy heart condition involving the septum and flow of blood.

Cartilage strong but pliable body tissue.

Cataract clouding of the eye lens.

Cherry eye prolapsed gland of the third eyelid.

Cleft palate improper growth of the two hard palates of the mouth.

Collie eye anomaly congenital defect of the back of the eye.

Congenital not the same as hereditary, but present at birth.

Congestive heart failure fluid buildup in lungs due to heart's inability to pump.

Conjunctivitis inflammation of the membrane that lines eyelids and eyeball.

Cow hocks poor rear legs that point inward; always incorrect.

Cryptorchid male animal with both testicles undescended.

Cushing's disease condition caused by adrenal gland's producing too much corticosteroid.

Cyst uninflamed swelling containing non-pus-like fluid.

Degeneration deterioration of tissue.

Demodectic mange red-mite infestation caused by *Demodex canis*.

Dermatitis skin inflammation.

Dewclaw a functionless digit found on the inside of a dog's leg.

Diabetes insipidus disease of the hypothalamus gland, resulting in animal's passing great amounts of diluted urine.

Diabetes mellitus excess glucose in blood stream.

Distemper contagious viral disease of dogs that can be most deadly.

Distichiasis double layer of eyelashes on an eyelid.

Dysplasia abnormal, poor development of a body part, especially a joint.

Dystrophy inherited degeneration.

Eclampsia potentially deadly disease in post-partum bitches due to calcium deficiency.

Ectropion outward turning of the eyelid; opposite of entropion.

Eczema inflammatory skin disease, marked by itching.

Edema fluid accumulation in a specific area.

Entropion inward turning of the eyelid.

Epilepsy chronic disease of the nervous system, characterized by seizures.

Exocrine pancreatic insufficiency body's inability to produce enough enzymes to aid digestion.

False pregnancy pseudo-pregnancy: bitch shows all signs of pregnancy but there is no fertilization.

Follicular mange demodectic mange.

Gastric dilatation bloat caused by the dog's swallowing air, resulting in a distended, twisted stomach; can be fatal.

Gastroenteritis stomach or intestinal inflammation.

Gingivitis gum inflammation caused by plaque buildup.

Glaucoma increased eye pressure affecting vision.

Heat stroke condition due to over-heating of an animal.

Hematemesis vomiting blood.

Hematoma blood-filled swollen area.

Hematuria blood in urine.

Hemophilia bleeding disorder due to lack of clotting factor.

Hemorrhage bleeding.

Heritable inherited, as in medical condition.

Hot spot moist eczema, characterized by dog's licking in same area.

Hyperglycemia excess glucose in blood.

Hypersensitivity allergy.

Hypertrophic cardiomyopathy left-ventricle septum becomes thickened and obstructs blood flow to heart.

Hypertrophic osteodystrophy condition affecting normal bone development.

Hypothyroidism disease caused by insufficient thyroid hormone.

Hypertrophy increased cell size, resulting in enlargement of organ.

Hypoglycemia glucose deficiency in blood.

Idiopathic disease of unknown cause.

IgA deficiency immunoglobin deficiency resulting in digestive, breathing and skin problems.

Inbreeding mating two closely related animals, e. g., mother–son.

Inflammation the changes that occur to a tissue after injury, characterized by swelling, redness, pain, etc.

Jaundice yellow coloration of mucous membranes.

Keratoconjunctivitis sicca dry eye.

Leukaemia malignant disease, characterized by white blood cells' being released into blood stream.

Lick granuloma excessive licking of a wound, preventing proper healing.

Merle coat color that is diluted.

Monorchid a male animal with only one testicle descended.

Neuritis nerve inflammation.

Nicitating membrane third eyelid pulling across the eye.

Nodular dermatofibrosis lumps on toes and legs, usually associated with cancer of kidney and uterus.

Osteochondritis bone or cartilage inflammation.

Outcrossing mating two breed representatives from different families.

Pancreatitis pancreas inflammation.

Pannus chronic superficial keratitis, affecting pigment and blood vessels of cornea.

Panosteitis inflammation of leg bones, characterized by lameness.

Papilloma wart.

Patellar luxation slipped kneecap, common in small dogs.

Patent ductus arteriosus an open blood vessel between pulmonary artery and aorta.

Penetrance frequency in which a trait shows up in offspring of animals carrying that inheritable trait.

Periodontitis acute or chronic inflammation of tissue surround the tooth.

Pneumonia lung inflammation.

Progressive retinal atrophy congenital disease of retina, causing blindness.

Pruritis persistent itching.

Retinal atrophy thin retina.

Seborrhea dry scurf or excess oil deposits on the skin.

Stomatitis mouth inflammation.

Tumor solid or fluid-filled swelling, resulting from abnormal growth.

Uremia waste product buildup in blood due to disease of kidneys.

Uveitis inflammation of the iris.

Von Willebrand's disease hereditary bleeding disease; lack of clotting factor.

Wall eye lack of color in the iris.

Weaning gradually separating the mother from her dependent nursing young.

Zoonosis animal disease that is communicable to humans.

INDEX

My Beagle

PUT YOUR PUPPY'S FIRST PICTURE HERE

Dog's Name _____

Date _____ Photographer _____